RECIPIENT OF THE 1986
C.L. SONNICHSEN BOOK AWARD

MURDER on the SANTA FE TRAIL

MURDER on the SANTA FE TRAIL

An International Incident, 1843

By MARC SIMMONS

THE UNIVERSITY OF TEXAS
AT EL PASO

FIRST EDITION
Library of Congress Catalog Card No. 86-051645
ISBN 87404-202-X

for
JAN, SUSAN
and JUDY

CONTENTS

PREFACE

MANY YEARS AGO in reading for the first time Josiah Gregg's *Commerce of the Prairies*, I became intrigued by his brief reference to a murder case that occurred on the Santa Fe Trail in 1843. The victim was Don Antonio José Chávez, scion of one of the wealthiest and most distinguished families of New Mexico. While traveling east on a buying trip to St. Louis, Don Antonio had been seized in central Kansas by a gang of outlaws who robbed and then shot him. The incident at once threw the American frontier into an uproar, not only on account of the brutality of the act, but also because it threatened to disrupt the profitable international trade carried on between Missouri and Mexico's province of New Mexico.

Later, as I developed an interest in Santa Fe Trail studies, I often came upon bits and pieces of information that provided details about the Chávez affair, beyond those supplied by Gregg. It was clear that the crime had been well publicized in its day and that it had serious diplomatic and economic repercussions. The victim, a citizen of Mexico, was slain on United States soil by desperados claiming a commission from the Republic of Texas. Thus, the interests of three nations were involved. The Chávez killing, I also discovered, was closely linked to two other well-known episodes in Southwestern history — the Warfield and Snively filibustering expeditions, both of which took place in 1843.

In spite of the importance of the case, historians have accorded it only passing notice. As I began to look into the matter more closely, at least one of the reasons quickly became apparent: the historical sources that would allow the full story to be stitched together are widely scattered and very thin. One of my early hopes was to locate the court records for those gang members who were brought to trial for the killing in April of 1844. Those papers, I felt certain, would fill in many of the details that are lacking at present. Unfortunately, I learned at the Kansas City Branch of the National Archives, where federal records for the region have been assembled, that judicial documents for the period I was investigating had largely been destroyed in the 1870s. A search revealed that the trial record was, indeed, gone. However, bills of indictment for the accused and other papers related to their arraignment, together with several documents dealing with reprieves and the final execution of two of the gang ringleaders, were uncovered.

For the rest I was obliged to ransack archival collections and comb printed sources looking for any stray mention of the Chávez murder that might shed added light. Archives of the Missouri Historical Society, St. Louis; the Historical Society of Missouri, Columbia; the Kansas State Historical Society, Topeka; and the New Mexico State Records Center, Santa Fe, proved particularly helpful. U.S. consular records in the National Archives illuminated diplomatic aspects of the case. Finally, a review of contemporary newspapers, most notably those published in St. Louis, plus the *New Orleans Weekly Picayune* and *Niles National Register*, permitted many gaps in the data to be closed.

Withal, parts of the case remain cloudy or mired in contradictions. But after eight years of gathering my information, the hour seemed to have arrived to put it all together and tell the tale. I was spurred on by the recollection of the character Mayhew in one of Maugham's short stories. He was an energetic industrialist who decided one day to leave his business and retire to the island of Capri, there to spend his time writing a history of the Roman Empire in the second century. For fourteen years he tirelessly assembled his sources and when they were all at hand, he sat down at his desk to write. But he had waited too long. He died and that vast accumulation of knowledge was lost forever. A like prospect should galvanize any writer.

It is likely that significant documents on the Chávez case will yet surface. Indeed, just as the present book was going to press, Professor Larry D. Ball published an article in the *Missouri Historical Review* on the murder trials, based upon a file of documents he had recently uncovered in the records of the Department of State. These papers, assembled as "Petitions for Pardons," contained excerpts from the missing trial records together with ancillary briefs. Providentially, this article came to my attention in time to incorporate its findings and correct several of my earlier conclusions.

In the future, even more information may become available. Perhaps buried in the papers of one of the Santa Fe traders who attended the St. Louis trials will be found his recollections of the testimony. Or maybe in the backfiles of some of the smaller Missouri newspapers there awaits discovery the text of the last speeches known to have been delivered on the scaffold by the two outlaws condemned to hang. Although a good deal, admittedly, is still missing, nevertheless, the narrative presented here pulls enough loose threads together to give a comprehensive picture of the entire episode, something that has not been done before. My purpose simply is to tell what happened when Don Antonio José Chávez went wheeling across the Santa Fe Trail and to explain how his misfortune fit into the larger scheme of Southwestern history.

I am pleased to acknowledge here the gracious assistance of the staffs of the several archives cited above. Pauline Fowler of Independence uncovered important information for me on the Gentry family in Missouri. William A. Goff provided clues that led to discovery of crucial documents in the Kansas City Branch of the National Archives. Thad Patterson, Seagraves, Texas, merits my thanks for furnishing details concerning the role of his ancestor, Rice Patterson, in the trials of the Chávez murderers. And a final word of gratitude must go to Susie Henderson for typing the manuscript under the assorted pressures that always seem to accompany the finishing of a book.

Marc Simmons
Cerrillos, New Mexico

INTRODUCTION

THE YEAR 1843 was one not soon forgotten along the western frontier of the United States. Those who believed in heavenly signs said the appearance of a comet, like a hazy star with a feathery tail, during late winter and early spring portended grave happenings in the months ahead. Remarkable cold and heavy snows lasted deep into March. Later, after the last frost, farmers began to notice a bumper crop of locust hatchlings and confidently predicted that '43 would be "the year of the locust." A plague of the insects had arrived with cyclical regularity every seventeen years since 1758, so that no one doubted another catastrophic visitation was at hand.

Winter's storms had deposited a massive snowpack on the upper Missouri River. The belated coming of warm weather, accompanied by drenching April rains, promoted a speedy melt and sent floodwaters cascading toward the Mississippi. Passengers on steamboats observed hundreds of trees falling into the river and saw submerged farmhouses with only the roofs visible above the muddy current. The overflow on smaller tributaries, particularly in eastern Kansas, took out the few bridges and imposed costly delays upon freight wagons departing for the markets of New Mexico. In fact, overland travel in every direction was seriously impeded.

In an era when an odd mix of religion and superstition guided the thought of the comman man, dire events inevitably were interpreted in supernatural terms. By coincidence a New York farmer and recent convert to the Baptist faith was waiting in the wings with a timely prophecy of doom that seemed to explain all. William Miller had examined Biblical data and calculated that the return of Christ and the end of the world would occur at 3 A.M. on 21 March 1843. His preachings, known as Millerism, were extensively reported and even occasionally ridiculed in the press. He attracted thousands of believers. The faithful at the final hour were to dress in bed sheets, properly termed ascension robes, and assemble in graveyards or on hilltops, there to await flying chariots that would transport them bodily to heaven.

Santa Fe trader Josiah Gregg, who was well educated and scorned popular delusions, tells us that many folk on the Missouri border believed that the comet and the unusual weather were signs of the fulfillment of Miller's prophecy.[1] To the relief of some and the disappointment of many more, the twenty-first of March came and went with no indication that it was Judgment Day. Miller hastily revised his caclulations, claiming an error, and set a new date. And, when that passed he set another, and after that another. In spite of unrealized expectations, the devoted Millerites clung to their faith. On one of the revised dates, 22 October 1844, much of the population of Boonville, Missouri, located at the original head of the Santa Fe Trail, climbed a river bluff and waited all night for earth's demise.[2]

Disasters, real and foreshadowed, were not the only events making news in that year of 1843. The trade with New Mexico was booming, having climbed to the value of half a million dollars annually since the trail to Santa Fe was opened in 1821. Little Franklin, in the bottoms across the Missouri from Boonville, had served as the first outfitting point, but when a flood washed it away in the latter 1820s, newly founded Independence, one hundred miles farther west, took over that role. The town's prosperity was already soaring as the great Oregon migration began in 1843, providing added economic stimulus.

Initially, the Santa Fe commerce had been the exclusive property of Missouri merchants who went forth each spring with a stock of goods, sold out at retail or wholesale, and returned home at summer's end with their profits. Before long, however, some of the leading men of New Mexico — members of old aristocratic families like the Chávezes, Armijos, Pereas, and Oteros — began to see that they were missing out on the large rewards going into the pockets of the Americans. Would it not be feasible, they wondered, to enter the yawning trade and corner a share of the market for themselves?

A step in that direction was taken in 1825 with the arrival in Santa Fe of Don Manuel Escudero, a wealthy merchant from Chihuahua City. Don Manuel was head of a trade caravan bound for the Missouri settlements where he intended to buy merchandise direct from wholesalers. Before starting out, Escudero was commissioned by New Mexican Governor Bartolomé Baca to arrange with U.S. authorities to open their borders to traders from Mexico. Escudero continued eastward to Franklin, becoming the first Mexican to conduct a wagon train over the Santa Fe Trail. Traveling on to St. Louis and Washington, he evidently met success in his overtures to the American government. At least we know that the following year, 1826, witnessed the initial entry of prominent New Mexicans into the Santa Fe trade.[3]

Their participation, meager at first, gradually expanded with the result that by 1843 it was conceded by observers on the scene that Mexicans from New Mexico and Chihuahua had become the majority among merchants, wagonmasters, and drovers involved in the overland traffic.[4] That fact, underscoring the international aspects of the business, gave the Santa Fe trade its own distinctive configuration and color.

The people of Missouri were not only acutely aware but also fully appreciative of the benefits they derived from the Mexican commerce. Theirs, like other undeveloped frontier states, suffered from a shortage of hard money, a condition that encouraged circulation of wildcat bank notes and counterfeit bills. The influx of Mexican silver pesos from Santa Fe and Chihuahua City had a stabilizing effect on the rural economy, and the Bank of Missouri, established in 1837, soon gained a reputation as one of the soundest state banks in the nation. The institution avoided a "run" in 1839 by the timely deposit of forty-five thousand dollars in pesos brought back by the returning merchant train.[5]

The profits in silver were not confined only to those directly engaged in trafficking on the trail. The business had a ripple effect that spread its benefits widely among the border communities. Departing caravans, be they American or Mexican, had need of a considerable variety of supplies and services. Farmers furnished food products and grain for the animals. Stock raisers found a ready demand for draft mules and oxen. Craftsmen of all kinds had no dearth of orders — blacksmiths, wheelwrights, wainwrights, carpenters who carved yokes, saddlers, harness makers, gunsmiths, and coopers. And, of course, small merchants dealing in everything from iron pots to canvas experienced brisk sales. The Mexican trade was a giant bonanza for Missouri's infant economy.

It is against this backdrop that the dramatic events surrounding the shooting of the New Mexican Chávez unfolded. In that unsettled spring when comets, inclement weather, floods, forecasts of locusts, and a rumored ending of the world were keeping citizens on edge, word of the crime spread new consternation and alarm. But in this instance, unlike the others, some human intervention was possible. The rapid and decisive response of Missourians to the fatal affair saw justice done and provided a satisfactory conclusion to the story that follows.

CHAPTER

I

THE VICTIM

IT IS LARGELY a matter of accident that Don Antonio José Chávez gained a small niche in the history of the Santa Fe Trail. By the manner of his death is he remembered at all. Had the stars been aligned in even a slightly different way, he would have missed his appointment with death in that fateful year of 1843 and been swallowed up in obscurity. But as it is, his personal history assumes some significance, as does the set of circumstances that led him to attempt a crossing of the plains from his home in the upper Rio Grande Valley to America's border state of Missouri.

The place and date of Antonio José's birth have thus far not come to light. Since it is known that several of his siblings were born on the Chávez estate at Los Padillas, down the Rio Grande from Albuquerque, it seems safe to assume that he too entered this world there. It is recorded that his elder brother Mariano's birthday was 8 December 1808, but how many years after that Antonio José was born is a matter for speculation. Josiah Gregg described him as "young Chávez" at the time of his murder on the trail, so it is perhaps reasonable to suggest that he was then in his late twenties.[1]

The parents of Antonio José were Francisco Xavier Chávez and Ana María Alvarez del Castillo. The father is best remembered as the first

1

governor of New Mexico after Mexican independence. He assumed office on 5 July 1822, succeeding the last Spanish governor, Don Facundo Melgares. The Chávezes were an old and distinguished family from Spain who had occupied prominent positions in New Mexico from the time of the founding of the province in 1598. By the early nineteenth century, they could be counted among the most prosperous of the *gente fina*, or upper class, with large land holdings, vast flocks of sheep, and extensive mercantile interests. By marriage they were closely allied to the handful of other patrician families who dominated political, social, and economic life in the provincial little world of the upper Rio Grande Valley.[2]

Antonio José had three brothers and five sisters. One of the brothers, Tomás, was sent at the age of twelve to be educated in Durango, Mexico. He never returned home, remaining there to become an eminent lawyer and judge and to marry a niece of Antonio de Zubiría, the bishop of Durango. The two other brothers, however, continued to reside on the family estate and in partnership with Antonio José became heavily involved in the overland trade.[3]

The eldest of these was Mariano José. He married Dolores Perea, daughter of a leading merchant family of Bernalillo, apparently sometime in the early 1830s. Their first son, José Francisco, was born on their hacienda of Los Padillas in 1833. He was destined to become a leading military and political figure in territorial New Mexico and, upon his assassination in 1904, the subject of one of the region's most baffling murder mysteries.[4]

In addition to Spanish, Mariano Chávez spoke English, French, and Latin. Included in a speech he delivered at Santa Fe in 1844 was a quote from the French writer and traveler Alexis de Tocqueville. These bits of information would indicate that he was well educated, perhaps, like his younger brother Tomás, sent during his youth to schools in Mexico. It is plausible to assume, therefore, that the two remaining brothers, Antonio José and José, were also the beneficiaries of a good education, something comparatively rare then in New Mexico.[5]

For much of his adult life, Mariano seems to have been involved in New Mexican politics, a role that came naturally to a man of his social status and whose father had been governor. In 1834 he was a member of the provincial deputation, or legislative body, and the following year he served briefly as acting governor. During the revolutionary disturbances of 1837, which resulted in the death of Governor Albino Pérez, he became a leader in the counter-revolutionary movement centered in the towns south of Albuquerque and, as second in command to his kinsman Manuel Armijo, was instrumental in restoring order.

A reorganization of the Mexican national government in 1843 resulted in the replacement of New Mexico's provincial deputation with a new departmental assembly. Mariano Chávez became the first president of the assembly and, at its initial meeting on 1 January 1844, delivered a patriotic speech. Two weeks later, when Governor Manuel Armijo resigned from office because of illness, Mariano once again assumed the acting governorship. His own health began to fail during the first half of 1845, obliging him to leave public office. He died on 18 June 1845.[6]

Antonio José's last brother, José Chávez (who often used his full surname, Chávez y Castillo, to distinguish himself from several other José Chávezes of the period), also held various political posts, including that of acting governor during the latter half of 1845. He was married to Manuela Armijo, while Antonio José wed her sister Barbara Armijo, they being nieces of Governor Manuel Armijo. It is interesting to note that in 1856, José's son Felipe (who would inherit the Chávez freighting business) married his first cousin, María Josefa, daughter of his uncle Antonio José. This practice of close intermarriage within the small upper class assisted in keeping family fortunes intact and political power concentrated in a few hands.[7]

What has been said thus far gives some idea of the influence and prestige of the three Chávez brothers. Each lived in his own house with wife and children on the huge Los Padillas estate. Mariano, being the elder, occupied the main residence with a private chapel that had belonged to their father. Eighteen-year-old Susan Magoffin, passing by with her merchant husband in 1846, the year after Mariano's death, described his adobe home as being very large and exceedingly neat and clean. The main *sala*, or receiving hall, she observed, was furnished "with handsome Brusseles carpet, crimson worsted curtains, with gilded rings and cornice, white marble slab pier tables — hair and crimson worsted chairs, candelabras. Eight or ten gilt-framed mirrors were all around the wall." Most, if not all, of these elegant appointments must have come by wagon over the Santa Fe Trail. Mariano's widow, Dolores Perea, met the Magoffins at the great door, and, according to Susan, "she was very polite, friendly, and invited us to spend some time with her. All was with true hospitality."[8]

The Chávez fortune which the three brothers worked assiduously to enlarge, was founded upon a variety of business enterprises. One was sheep raising, the mainstay of the New Mexican economy since colonial days. No data are available on the size of their flocks, but comparative figures from other raisers allow us to believe they were enormous. In 1832 New Mexico's combined sheep and goat population was almost a quarter of a million. A few years later, trader Josiah Gregg declared that sheep formed "the principal article of exportation."[9] With the Chávez merchant trains that traveled to the interior of Mexico, sheep were driven on the hoof by *peones* to be sold by the thousands in southern markets.

A second source of income derived from investments in mining, specifically in the gold placers located amid the Ortiz Mountains twenty miles south of Santa Fe. One writer claims that the controlling interests there were held by the Armijos, Chávezes, and Pereas. Most of the gold extracted was in the form of dust, flakes, and nuggets, and a significant portion of that evidently found its way over the trail to Missouri. When Antonio José Chávez departed for the East on his last trip, he had in his possession a leather pouch containing four pounds of gold dust, presumably from the Ortiz placers.[10]

The most lucrative activity of the Chávez brothers was in commerce — the freighting and wholesaling of goods from the United States to New Mexico over the Santa Fe Trail and from New Mexico to the interior of Mexico by way of the old *camino real*. Occasionally, they entrusted their caravans to faithful *mayordomos*, but more commonly one of the brothers took personal charge of management of the wagons. Like other New Mexicans committed to the overland trade, the Chávezes played the role of mercantile middlemen, buying American and European products in the United States, transporting them to New Mexico, and then reshipping them to Mexican markets below El Paso. The growth of this kind of international traffic from the 1830s onward opened new avenues to prosperity, allowing the Chávez family and others of the ruling elite to consolidate their hold on the provincial economy.

At one time or another before 1843, Mariano, José, and Antonio José all undertook trips east to make purchases from wholesalers and importers. Independence, located near the western border of Missouri, was then the main launching point for Santa Fe-bound caravans and could furnish whatever was needed in the line of draft stock, wagons, and trail equipment. The new community of Westport, eight miles to the west and close to the Kansas line, was just beginning its rise to prominence as a servicing point for outfitters. Although both places could offer domestic goods at wholesale to overland traders, the selection was comparatively limited and costly. For that reason, the Chávezes customarily left their wagons and crews in Independence, boarded a steamboat at the neighboring landing, and descended the Missouri River to St. Louis. As the great entrepôt for western commerce and the fur trade, that city was well supplied with merchandise of every description. Even so, on occasion when the prices were not to their liking, the Chávez brothers would continue on to markets in the East. They booked passage on a steamboat up the Ohio River to Pittsburgh, where some business could be transacted, thence went by stagecoach to the railhead of Chambersburg and there boarded a train for New York City. In New York they dealt principally with Peter Harmony, Nephews & Company, a firm which catered to the New Mexican traders and had among its clients Governor Manuel Armijo. Retracing their route, with purchases in tow, they saw to the loading of their wagons in Independence and completed the return journey to New Mexico.[11]

In the spring of each year, after the threat of prairie blizzards was past and the grass began to green, providing feed for livestock, Missouri merchants gathered at Independence to form what became known as the annual caravan to Santa Fe. The inconveniences of traveling in a large convoy — a slower pace and competition for grass and for water at some of the western springs — were largely offset by the security from Indian attack afforded in numbers. In a similar manner, New Mexicans and Chihuahuans found it convenient to assemble their own large caravans at Santa Fe in late April to cross the plains for a season of trading in *Los Estados*, The States. Unlike the Americans, they were frequently accompanied by members of their families.

The Chávezes by 1840 were usually represented in the eastbound convoy, but when business demanded, they were not adverse to forming their own smaller parties for a crossing of the trail at other times of the year. That was the case in September 1839 when José Chávez with five companions and their servants departed for Independence. No doubt it was personal influence that led Governor Armijo to provide a detachment of twenty-five soldiers to escort the travelers as far as the Mexican boundary on the Arkansas River.

Accompanying the New Mexicans was a lone American, Matthew C.

Field, a health-seeker and tourist who, having just concluded a pleasant interlude in Santa Fe, was returning home. In his account of the journey, he describes Don José as "a new speculator," and indicates that he spoke not a word of English nor "knew aught of the manners of the people" of the United States. At the village of San Miguel on the Pecos River, where he joined the group, Field recorded in his diary that he got out his grammar and taught old Don José his letters in English.[12] From Field's remarks it is plausible to conclude that this was José Chávez's maiden venture eastward, perhaps representing his family's entry into direct trade with American wholesalers.

The party reached Independence on 30 October, remained a few days, and then went down the Missouri on the steamer *Pizarro*, reaching St. Louis 11 November. The press reported that among the arrivals on the *Pizarro* were Matt Field and five Mexican gentlemen from Santa Fe who were bearers of sixty thousand dollars in specie.[13] During the winter José continued on to Philadelphia and New York making purchases of dry goods and hardware. Some of it must have been acquired on credit, for upon his return to Independence the following spring he had accumulated seventy-five thousand dollars' worth of merchandise.[14]

The annual caravan to Santa Fe that year, 1840, was a small one, apparently composed mainly of Mexican proprietors who, like José, had wintered in the East. He had a total of eleven wagons, the largest contingent in the train. An American is reported to have brought three wagons. That may have been Darby H. Cantrell, the man in charge of the entire caravan. There were delays and a start was not made until late May or early June. By 10 July, José Chávez was in Santa Fe where he paid twelve hundred dollars in duties to Mexican customs officials. That was at a rate less than half of what his American competitors were obliged to pay.[15]

Nowhere in the accounts of the 1840 caravan is there reference to the presence of Mariano Chávez. But in fact there is reason to believe that in the spring he had joined the first eastbound train, composed of forty wagons from Chihuahua and New Mexico, reaching Independence two weeks before his brother José left for home with his winter's gathering of goods. That Mariano accompanied him back to New Mexico is suggested by entries in the customs house records still preserved at Santa Fe. Therein, it is noted that on 10 July Mariano Chávez and on 11 July José Chávez were each issued *guías*, or mercantile passports, which were required of all persons doing business in the Mexican Republic.

Those documents indicate that both brothers had just arrived from the United States.[16]

The next month, August, José and his younger brother Antonio José obtained new *guías* allowing for travel to points south. Under Mexican law, such passports were mandatory for the transport of trade goods from one state to another. Their destinations were listed as the states of Chihuahua, Sonora, and Sinaloa. José Chávez was also cleared for travel to San Juan de Los Lagos in Jalisco, located fourteen hundred miles below New Mexico. A great trade fair was held there annually during the first twelve days of December, the Mexican government suspending the usual duties and sales taxes for the duration of the event. The fair, for that reason, was popular with traders from New Mexico and the United States.[17]

The bulk of the seventy-five thousand dollars in merchandise acquired in the East by José the previous winter must have gone with the brothers on this expedition to Mexico. To it they would have added a quantity of local New Mexican products, what were called *efectos del país*, which had a ready sale in the interior. Included in that category were buckskins, buffalo hides, piñon nuts, coarse wool cloth and serapes, stockings, leather moccasins, and sheep.[18]

These details regarding the commercial activities of the Chávez brothers for the years 1839-1840, while only of minor importance in themselves, do give us some idea of the dimensions and nature of that business. Their travels in pursuit of trade carried them halfway across the continent to markets on the east coast and, in another direction, far down into Mexico. Everywhere, in this early period, they were establishing useful contacts with wholesalers, merchants, and tradesmen who would continue to deal with Chávezes for the next several decades. The magnitude of the profits in those first years is unknown, owing to the failure of any business records to survive. But secondary evidence indicates that returns were substantial, and they showed a steady increase even after the deaths of Antonio José and Mariano in the 1840s. By the latter 1860s, José's son Felipe Chávez, who had assumed management of many of the family's interests, was reported to be a millionaire.[19]

During 1841 and 1842, that is, in the two years immediately preceding Antonio José's tragic last trip, information regarding travels of the Chávez brothers is sparse. The spring, 1841, eastbound train to Independence, composed of twenty-two wagons and bearing almost two hundred thousand dollars in specie, included "a company of about twenty Spanish Mexicans," among whom was one named Chávez. That would probably have been either José or Antonio José. The same Chávez was in the return caravan that departed Independence the following 11 October with thirty wagons carrying seventy-two tons of merchandise. That train arrived back in New Mexico on the heels of Governor Manuel Armijo's capture of the Texan Santa Fe Expedition, and the capital was still much astir over the episode.[20]

For the following year of 1842, no specific reference has yet come to light of a Chávez traveling to the United States. But likely one of the brothers was in the spring caravan and among the six Mexican traders known to have continued on to Pittsburgh "for the purpose of making contracts for waggons [sic], harness, & purchasing other articles."[21]

As the year 1843 dawned, it is easy to imagine that Mariano, José, and Antonio José held council at Los Padillas and laid plans for the coming season's trade. Business was flourishing, the volume of their freighting was on the increase, and the future loomed bright. Only one shadow darkened the horizon, a persistent rumor that Texan raiders were gathering on the western end of the Santa Fe Trail for the purpose of attacking Mexican shipping.

First reports of the danger had reached New Mexico as early as the previous October. As the acting U.S. consul in Santa Fe, Manuel Alvarez, informed the American secretary of state: "A body of lawless men had banded together upon the headwaters of the Arkansas and Platt rivers, calling themselves Texians, but they were thought only to be a band of robbers, & little or no account was taken of them." The matter became of graver concern the following January when Governor Manuel Armijo received notice that Colonel Charles A. Warfield, said to be of the Texan Army, had assumed command of this gang and was awaiting further reinforcements from the Republic. According to what Alvarez was able to learn, Warfield's "intention was to concentrate at the point at which the Santa Fe road crosses the Arkansas, with the view of plundering the caravans from Mexico to the U.S."[22]

This news occasioned considerable alarm, the more so when the suspicion arose that some sympathetic Americans in New Mexico were serving as spies for Warfield and were planning to slip him information regarding wagon trains taking their leave for Missouri. Governor Armijo was so concerned over that possibility that he ordered Americans living in the department to come to Santa Fe and undergo questioning by the authorities. At the same time he brushed aside complaints by

Consul Alvarez that the summons would cause "much trouble and vexation to many . . . innocent & inoffensive citizens."[23]

Josiah Gregg, chief chronicler of the trail for this period, contends that the anxiety quickly subsided and the New Mexican merchants concluded that it had been another example "of those rumors of Texan invasion which had so often spread useless consternation through the country."[24] That, indeed, may have been the view of the Chávez brothers as they busily arranged plans for travel. They may have also felt that they had nothing to fear from Texans, since in the past they had shown themselves as not unsympathetic to that people. Two years before, Mariano had displayed special kindness to the prisoners of the Texan Santa Fe Expedition by furnishing them a considerable quantity of provisions and blankets. Afterward, when the captives were started on a brutal march south to a lockup in Mexico, Mariano's wife Dolores Perea had crossed the Rio Grande from Los Padillas and "administered comforts" to some of the most needy in the cavalcade.[25] Moreover, it was widely known that the Chávezes were often at odds with their kinsman, Governor Armijo, who in Texas was regarded as the chief villain in the mistreatment of their prisoners.

It was Gregg's claim that the Chávezes represented "a family whose liberal principles could not otherwise have been very unfavorable to Texas."[26] If that was true, then the brothers might have been counting upon their reputation and name to keep them out of harm's way on the Santa Fe Trail. Unfortunately, it proved to be a serious miscalculation.

This was the plan hatched at Los Padillas: in late February Antonio José would leave Santa Fe for the East accompanied by only a small group of companions and servants. On 1 April, José and his son José Francisco, who was to enter a Jesuit school in St. Louis, would follow by joining the regular spring caravan composed of Mexicans as well as some Americans who had wintered in New Mexico. This much is known for a certainty. What is missing is the motive for Antonio José's early departure, which under the best of circumstances would have been hazardous.

The safest guess is that he intended to make a flying trip to St. Louis or even beyond, amass a quantity of merchandise, and have it back in Independence by May in time to join the annual American caravan bound for Santa Fe. That would leave José, arriving in Independence by the later eastbound train, the opportunity to conduct other Chávez business at a more leisurely pace through the summer. Whatever Antonio José's motive, whether this or some other, it must have been a compelling one to prompt him to travel the trail as he did in the face of several known perils.

One of those was the inclemency of the season. Veteran traders, where possible, avoided crossing the plains in winter for they knew all too well the risks involved in encountering a major snowstorm in open country. The consequences of such an event had been made manifestly clear two years before. Manuel Alvarez and a small company had been journeying toward Missouri in November when they were caught by a blizzard at Cottonwood Creek in eastern Kansas. The violence of the wind, which continued unabated for forty-eight hours, prevented the kindling of a campfire, and the snow accumulated to a depth of three feet. Two men froze to death, the others suffered frostbite, and most of the animals perished. The disaster would have been greater had not Alvarez forced his way through the storm to Independence and sent back a rescue party.[27]

Antonio José exposed himself to a second serious hazard when he decided to set forth on the trail in a small body. True, the threat from Indians was somewhat diminished at that time of the year since the Plains tribes stayed close to their winter camps in the timbered river bottoms. But there was always the chance of running upon one of those camps or of meeting a stray hunting party. Such an unlooked-for encounter could prove fatal to travelers few in number.

And finally there was the risk posed by the Texan marauders. As noted, the Chávezes may have discounted the threat from that quarter. Even so, Antonio José chose to follow the more southerly Cimarron Cutoff of the Santa Fe Trail, since reports placed the Texans on the Mountain Branch farther north. It is a matter of record that the main caravan from Santa Fe, which set out 1 April, also took the southern route so as to avoid Colonel Warfield and his raiders.[28]

Contemporary accounts vary with regard to the size of the party that escorted Antonio José on his journey. Josiah Gregg, who had access to firsthand information, stated that he left "with but five servants, two wagons, and fifty-five mules."[29] Most later writers accepted his statement. However, American newspapers which subsequently reported upon Antonio José's misfortune declared that he had started with twenty men. After bitter winter weather caused frostbite in the ranks and killed most of the mules, fifteen men deserted and returned to New Mexico. This occurred on the open plain (or Jornada) between the Cimarron and Arkansas rivers. At that point, Chávez had to abandon one of his wagons and, hitching his surviving mules to the other, he continued on with the remaining five members of his party.[30]

Santa Fe freighter "Uncle Dick" Wootton, speaking many years after the fact, said that Antonio José "traveled by carriage in the old Spanish style, with outriders and all that sort of thing."[31] Colonel Henry Inman, in a general history of the trail published at the end of the century, wrote that Chávez had "a private coach, several servants and other retainers."[32] Although both men were reporting from hearsay, it would appear highly possible that the party did indeed include a carriage, at least in the beginning. But, if so, after the loss of the mules to severe weather, it too must have been abandoned, along with the one wagon.

Just the year before, Consul Alvarez had noted in his diplomatic correspondence that it was extremely dangerous to cross the trail with a company as small as fifteen men.[33] But now after the desertion, Antonio José was reduced to a party far below that. Yet, he apparently gave no thought to turning back, and as he pushed onward through the biting cold of central Kansas, he must have had every expectation of arriving safely at last in Independence.

New Mexico Governor Manuel Armijo who was heavily involved in the Santa Fe trade at the time of the murder of Antonio José Chávez. (Museum of New Mexico Neg. No. 50809)

CHAPTER

II

THE PLOT

THE CHAIN OF EVENTS that led up to the slaying of Antonio José Chávez can be said to have had its origin in the assorted antagonisms and conflicts that had arisen in the previous decade between Mexicans and American settlers in Texas. At first, in the 1820s, the Republic of Mexico had welcomed the energetic and industrious colonists from the north and granted them large tracts of empty agricultural land in the eastern sections of the Texas province. But as the migration became a flood, worried officials attempted to slow the entry of foreigners and impose new restrictions and regulations upon those already arrived. These steps, together with a growing perception of the capriciousness and instability of the government in Mexico City, propelled the Texans into open rebellion in 1835. The swift but bitterly fought movement for independence culminated at the Battle of San Jacinto, 21 April 1836.

The launching of the Republic of Texas was anything but auspicious. A newly installed government proved weak and unsure, the treasury teetered on the brink of bankruptcy, hostile Indians assailed the settlements almost at will, and perhaps most pressing of all was the threat of a new invasion by Mexico, which refused to acknowledge loss of her territory. Mirabeau B. Lamar, who succeeded Sam Houston as president late in 1838, tackled several of the problems head-on. He mounted a campaign to expel all Indians from Texas, tried to get loans from

European nations, and attempted to expand boundaries of the Republic westward. This last venture resulted in the disastrous Texan Santa Fe Expedition of 1841. Lamar sent a force of 321 men to New Mexico with the intention of asserting claim over that Mexican province and, failing that, to try and divert at least a portion of the lucrative Santa Fe trade toward Texas.

Mismanaged from the start, the expedition lost its way on the plains and by the time the eastern settlements of New Mexico came in sight the men were bordering on starvation and thoroughly demoralized. Governor Manuel Armijo, calling out his troops, had little difficulty in rounding up the invaders, who were promptly set on a brutal march that ended with imprisonment in Mexico City. The affair had two immediate consequences. First it sparked a heated diplomatic controversy between Mexico and the United States, when the latter intervened to win release of the captives. Second, it further inflamed Texan sentiment against Mexico, the more so when George Wilkins Kendall, a New Orleans newspaperman who had accompanied the abortive expedition as an observer, published a vivid account of the participants' sufferings.

Late in 1841 Sam Houston soundly defeated Lamar in a new presidential election. Within a few months, he was confronted with a serious threat from the south when Mexican troops began to stage raids across the Rio Grande. The most serious incident occurred in midsummer as General Adrian Woll, a French soldier of fortune employed by the Mexican army, briefly seized San Antonio and then retreated with a number of prominent Texas prisoners in tow. A small retaliatory force that went in pursuit was subsequently overwhelmed at the Mexican town of Mier. Seventeen of its members were later executed and the remainder were dispatched as prisoners to the south.

While these events provide a backdrop for the Chávez murder and help explain an act of Sam Houston that was soon to set in motion the slide toward that tragedy, the career of another man, Charles Warfield by name, must be examined to find immediate causes. For it is with Warfield and his mercenary activities that the fate of Chávez was sealed.

The son of a successful New Orleans merchant, Charles Alexander Warfield seems to have been well educated and highly literate. A story in the Houston *Morning Star* spoke of him glowingly as "Connected with some of the most respectable families of Louisiana, and [demonstrating] an irreproachable character."[1] His own hometown newspaper in 1843 referred to him as "a young man of most excellent character and reputably connected in this city."² During the ten years prior to that date he had ranged widely through the Rocky Mountains as a trapper, and after 1839 lived for a time in New Mexico. He paid at least one visit to Texas, the circumstances of which are unknown, and he was in Missouri with enough frequency that some sources mistakenly refer to him as a Missourian. His presence there was tied to his commercial interests in the Santa Fe trade. Irish artist Alfred S. Waugh had a chance meeting with Warfield at New Orleans in 1844 and wrote that he was "an agreeable acquaintance, full of anecdote and incident of travel, which he relates with much interest. He is a young man of good appearance, agreeable manners and pleasant wit. Among the Indians he was known as Wa-pes-ta or White Plume, for his habit of wearing a white feather in his hat."³

These few details suggest the picture of a bright and resourceful individual, full of enthusiasm and daring, who was seriously afflicted with wanderlust, one who unquestionably rated the title of adventurer. There was also a strong element of romanticism in his nature, a trait that perhaps more than any other illuminates his motives and actions. As a corollary to that, it would not be inaccurate to state that he was basically honorable in his intentions, a quality found often in those who incline toward a romantic view of life. Devotion to honor, however, is no guarantee that clouded vision will not obscure the path to right conduct, as Warfield's case amply proves.

In July 1842, Colonel William A. Christy of New Orleans, a close personal friend of Sam Houston, wrote the Texas president a letter that outlined a bold scheme. The central figure in the plan was Christy's acquaintance Charles Warfield who proposed to form and lead an expedition of volunteers to overthrow the provincial governments in New Mexico and Chihuahua and win the allegiance of their populations for Texas. Further, Warfield offered his services at no cost and agreed to split all booty seized with the financially strapped Republic. Evidently, his recent experience in northern Mexico had convinced him that the design could be carried out, even though its similarities to Lamar's ill-conceived Texan Santa Fe Expedition should have made him wary of predictions. One thing he asked for in his dealing with Houston was strictest secrecy. That, he believed, would leave him freer to recruit volunteers, to the number of five hundred to one thousand men.⁴ Christy, acting as intermediary, gave the plan and Warfield his strong personal recommendation.

That support was enough to convince Sam Houston. In replying to Colonel Christy he emphasized that the Warfield Expedition must be conducted upon the principles of "civilized and honorable warfare." And as to the fitness of Warfield to represent Texas, he added: "The character rendered of him by you is all the guaranty which I require."[5] It now seems strange that a matter of some diplomatic delicacy was handled by the president in such a casual manner.

Evidently Houston saw in the operation an opportunity to achieve any one of several possible aims — the acquisition of New Mexico, diversion of a portion of the Santa Fe trade to Texas, and, at the very least, the extracting of sweet revenge should Warfield manage to inflict even minimal punches against Mexico and its citizens. Such punishment, in his view, would serve as just retaliation for the recent Mexican forays north of the Rio Grande. Added to everything else was Warfield's promise to return half his spoils to the Texas treasury. A realistic appraisal of the chances of success for any of this must have indicated to Houston how dim prospects actually were, but Christy was a trusted friend, there was no cost and little risk in going ahead (or so he thought), and hence he gave his nod of approval.

In reality, the president did more than that. He instructed his Secretary of War and Marine George W. Hockley to issue Warfield appropriate authorization to carry out his invasion under the flag of the Republic. In conformity with Warfield's desire for secrecy, Hockley took action without informing other members of the government or seeking sanction from Congress. That became an important point later when things went awry, with the Chávez murder, and attempts were made to deny the responsibility of Texas. Notwithstanding, it is clear that Charles Warfield sought and received a legitimate commission from the Republic.

In August 1842, Secretary Hockley wrote Warfield a letter containing a statement of his authority and instructions, together with a commission as colonel in the service of Texas. Several points in the letter would be seen afterward to bear directly upon the Chávez case. For one, Colonel Warfield was empowered to commission junior officers to serve under him, the names of whom were to be forwarded to the Department of War for confirmation. For another, the secretary took pains to emphasize the lawfulness of the undertaking. "A just retribution . . . for injuries and cruelties inflicted by an enemy, is always legitimate warfare. Such retribution you are required to take; and from your high character and standing at home, it is scarcely deemed necessary to enjoin that the strictest regard will be paid to the . . . rules of warfare by *all* in the command." Plainly Hockley was concerned about the moral implications of the upcoming campaign, as he well might have had reason to be.

One other small point, seemingly unimportant at the time, was to have significant repercussions. Hockley granted Warfield complete discretion in determining the number of men to be enlisted and indicated in his letter that he had no idea as to where they were to come from. Colonel Warfield, in fact, had every intention of recruiting within the boundaries of the United States, a bit of information that he had neglected to mention to anyone.

Hockley's letter of instructions and commission were sent to New Orleans in care of William Christy, for the secretary had no knowledge of Warfield's address, nor was he, or for that matter President Houston, ever to have personal contact with the man. That appears all the more strange when it is understood that in case Warfield turned out to be anything less than the noble adventurer he had been represented, then Hockley was handing him a blank check for banditry. With no more than Christy's claim that Warfield "entertained good feelings toward the Texas cause," and wished to "engage in special service under its flag," the secretary and the president were willing to extend him broad powers and a military title.[6]

Since Charles Warfield was not a Texan, and hence could scarcely have been motivated by patriotism, it must be assumed that he entered into this affair for profit, and perhaps even more, for the pure love of excitement. Upon receiving the authorization from Hockley, he publicly announced his plan in New Orleans (a curious reversal on his part, since he had placed such value on secrecy in his dealings with Texas). At the same time he declared his resolve to fix a limit of ten thousand dollars on his share of the expected booty.[7]

Recruitment began at once. The record is not clear, but there is some shadowy evidence that the colonel may have traveled initially to Texas in a search for volunteers. In any case, one writer asserts that "he took it for granted that at least three hundred men would respond from Texas."[8] Warfield next may have gone hunting recruits in Arkansas before landing in St. Louis, the first location in which his drum beating can be firmly established. There he wrote letters, purchased equipment, and attempted to win over adherents. Contacts he had made earlier in the overland trade must have been of use to him now. So open were his activities that the local press could report afterward that he had exhibited blank commissions in the Texas military service and extended "the promise of office and rewards under the Texan Government," by which it was thought that he had "induced many persons on the frontier to engage in his enterprise."[9]

Whether Warfield actually attracted any substantial support in the St. Louis area remains doubtful, press reports notwithstanding. Later in October of 1842, he crossed the state to Independence and Westport at the head of the Santa Fe Trail where he resumed his quest for followers. Here he met with more success.

Among the first to be attracted by the colonel's blandishments were two brothers, John and David McDaniel, residents of Liberty in Clay County, which lay on the north bank of the Missouri River. John was said to have spent time in Texas where, after serving in the militia, he had turned to outlawry and reputedly committed several killings. Virtually nothing else is known of the brothers' background, other than that they were spoken of as "young men of good family." The lack of information is an unfortunate circumstance since John was to become the chief villain in the Chávez murder. His conduct later after his trial suggests that he may have been afflicted with a psychological disorder. But on the other hand, he simply might have possessed a badly flawed moral character. Such persons often are adept at covering their true natures by cunning manipulation and a feigned charm. If that was the pose of John McDaniel, then Colonel Warfield was completely taken in. Using one of his blank commissions, he enrolled the Missourian as a captain in the service of Texas.

On 30 October, Warfield departed Westport for the Rockies with a single companion, mountain man Tim Goodale. There is reason to believe he had managed to sign up fifty to sixty men, and these he now left in Captain McDaniel's charge, with instructions to continue recruiting.[10] It was Warfield's plan to spend the winter in the mountains and attempt to enlist another unit from among the comrades of his trapping days. With this force he would return east on the Santa Fe Trail as far as a small Point of Rocks (located on the Arkansas River just west of present Dodge City) where on 15 May 1843 he told McDaniel to meet him with the Missouri contingent. Warfield, in addition, may have counted upon rendezvousing with still another unit of men from Texas, numbering in its ranks, according to one newspaper of the day, some of those who had participated in the ill-starred Texan Santa Fe Expedition and were only recently released from prison in Mexico.[11] Presumably, they were out for revenge.

The Point of Rocks, the link-up site, was conveniently situated near the beginning of Mexican territory. As he must have carefully explained to McDaniel before leaving Westport, Warfield had in mind to prey upon Mexican caravans headed for their spring buying in Missouri, and when all possible profit had been wrung from that activity, to continue southwestward on his larger mission — the invasion of New Mexico. All of this was to be accomplished with the five hundred to one thousand men the colonel earlier had predicted would rally to his call. At the 15 May rendezvous he expected to see the culmination of his months of preparation and the commencement of the military phase of his scheme.

John McDaniel had five months to fill out his ranks, during the slow winter time in Westport, and be ready to march toward the Point of Rocks with the coming of spring. As it happened, not only did he fail to swell the number of enlistees, but those that Warfield is supposed to have attracted before his leaving, seem to have largely melted away. McDaniel's manifest lack of leadership qualities coupled with an arrogant and callous manner probably were obvious, even at this early stage, furnishing one cause for his failure to gather and hold support. Another was that his plans, as he voiced them, had taken on a sinister tone, sounding suspiciously like a venture in land piracy. Colonel Warfield, by contrast, had spoken in high and lofty phrases and conveyed the impression that his was a legitimate campaign strictly bound by the accepted rules of warfare. In taking that course, he was following the injunction given him by Secretary of War Hockley. Unhappily, he neglected to pay sufficient heed to another part of those instructions which required him to see that the officers under him also adhered to those rules.

The precise details of what Captain McDaniel did on the Missouri border that winter are not available. But in general, matters seem to have evolved in this way: after his failure at mass recruitment, he gathered around him a small corps of fourteen men who gave every indication of being willing to engage in blatant banditry on the Santa Fe Trail. Unlike Warfield, who was animated at least in some measure by "a sympathy for the Texas cause," these individuals displayed no interest in a patriotic crusade. They were drawn solely by promises of booty — easy pickings from poorly defended Mexican caravans, as Captain McDaniel airily represented them.

Owing to the publicity that ensued, and the legal proceedings, the names of all members of the "gang" have been preserved. They were:

John and David McDaniel, Joseph Brown, William Mason, Thomas Towson, Schuyler Oldham, brothers Gallatin and Christopher Searcy, Samuel O. Berry (or O'Berry), Nathaniel H. Morton, Benjamin F. Tolbert (or Talbert, or Tallbott), William F. Harris and his brother, "Doctor" Benjamin T. Harris, John McCormick, and Dr. Joseph R. De Prefontaine.[12] The McDaniels, Mason, Oldham, and the Searcy brothers came from Clay County, while the others are believed to have resided in neighboring Jackson County at either Independence or Westport. Up to the hour of their conversion to trail robbery, they seem to have been respected citizens, and indeed several were regarded as pillars of the community.

The most conspicuous in that respect was Dr. Prefontaine, the one figure in this company about whose background something is known. In 1836 he arrived in St. Louis and began the practice of medicine. Described as "a gentleman of culture," he also made an unsuccessful attempt at theatrical management. Evidently he had a quirky personality for in 1838 the proprietor of the Theater Bar threw him out of the establishment "for rolling on the floor, singing, and generally interfering with a performance of *Hamlet*."[13] The doctor avenged himself by attacking the Theater in the newspapers. Shortly, he left for western Missouri, stopping first at Lone Jack, a community southeast of Independence, and then moving on to the new village of Westport, close to the Kansas border.

There in 1839 he purchased four acres from John C. McCoy, the man who had platted and founded the townsite just seven years before. On this land Dr. Prefontaine built a house to accommodate his large family. Surviving business records of the Ewing and Clymer store disclose that he owed a running bill for ladies' and children's clothing.[14] That he had pretentions to gentility is indicated by the quality of some of the furnishings of his new residence: eight Windsor chairs, a mahogany buffet, a cherry bureau, and a library of rare books.[15] Such luxury at that early date was not common on the raw Missouri frontier.

During the summers of 1838 and 1840, the doctor worked for the Indian Department giving smallpox vaccinations to assorted tribes settled in the Indian reserve and around missions just across the line in Kansas.[16] Since the government had authorized only two hundred dollars for that work in 1840, Prefontaine must have regarded it as a mere supplement to the fees from his regular practice.

To this point nothing has been said that would suggest the doctor had any reason to join forces with a rogue like John McDaniel. Celebrated mountain man Richens "Uncle Dick" Wootton recalled many years later having made the brief acquaintance of Prefontaine, who, he remarked, "was one of the most prominent men in Jackson County."[17] And a news editor in St. Louis, who had known him there, described him as "one of the keenest, shrewdest, and most plausible men we ever met."[18]

But in spite of a well-polished image, the doctor was not all that he pretended to be, as his neighbors began to discover. His taste for luxuries and the costly demands of family life had drawn him into financial difficulties, and the means he adopted to solve the dilemma were not of the sort to win community approval.

One of his ploys, as revealed in the Jackson County Court records, was to buy property and simultaneously plaster it with mortgages. The county documents also show that he regularly presented a large doctor's bill at the settlement of almost every estate that came before the court, whether he had been the attending physician or not.[19] These artifices, however, failed to save him from ruin. On 12 February 1842 his house and acreage were lost to foreclosure to satisfy a mortgage of seven hundred dollars. His elegant furniture, library, and twelve other lots of items were ordered to be sold "at public outcry in the town of Westport to the highest bidder for ready money."[20] Prefontaine's reaction to this disaster, whether anger or remorse, is not known. But at minimum it can be said that his loss must have led him to explore every path offering some hope for recovery of his fortunes.

In the absence of specifics, the best guess is that Dr. Prefontaine first met John McDaniel at the Yoacham Tavern, a popular Westport gathering spot that served the captain as a place of recruitment and later as a rendezvous from which he and his company set forth on their errand of mischief.[21] As did the others who joined, Prefontaine was seduced by a vision of quick riches — to be gotten through unsavory means, certainly, but palliated by the color of legality which McDaniel's Texas commission, courtesy of Warfield, seemed to bestow.

The Yoacham Tavern, thus, assumes a role of some importance in this story, while its proprietor, Daniel Yoacham, figures as one of the minor players in the tragedy that ensued. He was among the first settlers of Westport, having migrated earlier from Tennessee with his wife Rosannah May who was a granddaughter of John Sevier, the first governor of that state. Daniel built a log home near the center of the budding hamlet and because he and Rosannah were hospitable by nature, travelers passing by found shelter under their roof. Before long, the Yoacham residence was doubling as a tavern, hostelry, and store.

At the beginning, the tavern had a large main room equipped with a bar, shelves, and a counter for merchandise. Later, as the business prospered, Daniel added a second story with an outside gallery. Notable among his guests were John C. Frémont, Kit Carson, Daniel Morgan Boone, and elders of the Mormon Church. He also served two terms as justice of the peace, dabbled in real estate, and bought and sold livestock. In every way Daniel Yoacham was an esteemed member of the community.

The accepted view has been that while John McDaniel sat at a table in the tavern's barroom hatching his plot and interviewing prospective confederates, Daniel Yoacham remained ignorant of the plans and the ominous turn they were taking. That, of course, is a bit hard to swallow given the fact that McDaniel was making no effort to conceal his intentions. The tavern keeper was well acquainted with several of the gang, particular Dr. Prefontaine, and the possibility exists that he lent some material support to the enterprise, without quite understanding where matters were going. His seemingly unwitting participation in one of the later stages of the crime lends weight to that interpretation.[22]

Another point of debate has to do with whether John McDaniel while in Westport had learned that Antonio José Chávez was traveling east on the Santa Fe Trail and at once began preparations to waylay him, or whether he started out to meet Warfield as planned, met the don by accident, and on the spur of the moment determined to rob him. Colonel Henry Inman, a plainsman with wide experience, took the former position in his book, *The Old Santa Fe Trail*. He claims that McDaniel's land pirates were fully aware of Chávez's approach and of the fact that on his annual comings he always carried considerable specie. While acknowledging that the gang's principal aim was to join Warfield, Inman says that they had already decided to make Chávez their victim along the way, and to that end they sent spies ahead on the trail.[23]

That the crime was premeditated, the result of a plot conceived in Westport, was also the belief of "Uncle Dick" Wootton. As he remembered it, "they [the gang] found out in some way when Chávez was coming through on one of his trips and went out to meet him in the Indian territory [i.e., Kansas], where there was very little law and where they seem to have thought they could commit any sort of crime with impunity."[24] This or a similar explanation finds echo in numerous

Yoacham's Tavern in Westport, Missouri, rendezvous of the McDaniel gang. (Author's photo, from an early drawing)

other accounts, many of them secondary, so that it is now difficult to judge how much Captain McDaniel may or may not have known about the movements of Don Antonio.

In the long run the question becomes academic, for whether the McDaniel party encountered Chávez by design or by accident, the melancholy results would have been the same. About 1 April, John and David McDaniel at the head of thirteen other men left Yoacham's Tavern under the flimsy pretext of embarking on a buffalo hunt. Starting out across the wide prairies, they followed the deeply scored ruts of the Santa Fe Trail.[25] None of them could know that for all concerned it would prove an excursion into disaster.

CHAPTER III

THE CRIME

WELL MOUNTED and in high spirits, members of the McDaniel company pushed out into eastern Kansas, averaging about thirty miles a day. Behind them they had left a frontier community filled with anxiety, for word of their intentions had passed from house to house and from farm to farm across Jackson and into neighboring counties. Several of Warfield's early recruits, who quit the movement when belligerent John McDaniel had taken charge, disclosed some of the plans for raiding, and the gossip mill was further fueled by those who overheard loud and unguarded talk of the plotters in the barroom at Yoacham's Tavern. Thus, it had become common knowledge that the band meant to attack the annual Mexican caravan due shortly from Santa Fe. That prospect, with its threat of disruption in the valuable overland trade, was pleasing to no one in western Missouri.

The town of Independence by this date was acknowledged as the foremost outfitting point for the merchants and freighters involved in the Santa Fe commerce. And it was there that the activities of Warfield and McDaniel stirred the greatest alarm. As a consequence, leading citizens composed a letter on 13 March, more than two weeks before the gang's departure from Westport, addressing it to the superintendent of Indian Affairs for the West, D. D. Mitchell, whose office was in

St. Louis. In it they warned him that McDaniel's "banditti" were planning to enter the Indian country beyond the Missouri border for illegal purposes.[1]

At this time all of the southern plains below the Platte River and extending west to lands claimed by Mexico and the Texas Republic were vaguely defined as the Indian Territory. Into this arid and largely treeless country, then thought to be unfarmable and thus uninhabitable by white men, had been shunted the remnants of several dozen tribes displaced from their original homes in the East. Through subagents, Superintendent Mitchell from St. Louis presided over the various Indian groups and saw to the distribution of their yearly government annuities. Moreover, in the absence of any established federal administration in that vast domain, he exercised civil authority in cooperation with the army which exercised police powers. It was for that reason that the people of Independence directed their information and expressed their worries to him.

In spite of the obvious urgency of the situation, Mitchell reacted slowly to the news reaching him from the frontier. It was more than a month later that he addressed a letter to Secretary of War James M. Porter, on 21 April 1843. In it he made no mention of the concerns of Independence residents over the departure of McDaniel, but he did say that information reaching him from various sources cast new light on a dark subject, to wit, the movements of Colonel Warfield in the Texas service.

Said Mitchell to the secretary: "Warfield disclaims all intention to rob or interfere with the citizens of the United States, but contends that he has a right, according to international law, to rob the citizens of Mexico who may be met with on the route between frontiers of Missouri and Santa Fe, provided they are not within the limits of the United States.

"Under this plausible view of the subject, he has been enabled to enlist a great number of well-disposed men, who would have spurned all propositions of *what they conceived to be unlawful.*" (Emphasis his.) Nowhere in these words is there expressed any great sense of alarm. By them, the superintendent managed to convey the impression that he was nothing more than an unimaginative bureaucrat, incapable of recognizing a crisis that had encamped on his own doorstep. To Secretary Porter in Washington he ended by saying, "It is not for *me* to give an opinion on the subject." And he adds that the details about

Warfield in his letter are "given merely for the information of the government."[2] In other words, Mitchell was unwilling to rock the boat of bureaucracy, even to the extent of issuing a warning or making a recommendation.

In reality the course of events had already rushed far past the point where intervention of any kind by the Indian superintendent would have made a difference. For by 21 April, the date of Mitchell's letter, John McDaniel and his not-so-well-disposed men had resolutely entered upon the side road that led to their brief but brutal jaunt into criminality.

As observed earlier, some question exists as to whether Captain McDaniel, in going to join Warfield, encountered Chávez by chance or whether, having learned of his approach, planned in Westport to ambush him. One other possibility, regarding McDaniel's intentions on the trail, was widely reported in the western press at the time. According to these accounts, both the Warfield and the McDaniel expeditions were as eager to intercept the spring westbound caravan leaving from Independence as they were the eastbound wagons coming from Santa Fe. In the former, known to be accompanying the usual contingent of American merchants, were two young New Mexicans, identified only as a nephew of Governor Manuel Armijo and a relative of Captain Damasio Salazar. It was Salazar who two years before had conducted the Texan Santa Fe Expedition prisoners to El Paso on the first leg of their journey to imprisonment in central Mexico. The story of his cruelty had earned him the undying hatred of all Texans, and even the Mexican press denounced his conduct as an act of barbarism.[3]

The pair of youths had come to the States the year before as agents for their kinsmen and in New York had purchased goods that in the case of Manuel Armijo amounted to an investment of eighteen thousand to twenty thousand dollars. In July they saw to the loading of this stock on the steamboat *Lebanon* at St. Louis and then began the voyage up the Missouri to Independence and the head of the Santa Fe Trail. Unfortunately, about fifty miles below its destination, the *Lebanon* sank in five feet of water with loss of all merchandise aboard. When Governor Armijo at Santa Fe heard of the misfortune he flew into a rage. The U.S. consul there, Manuel Alvarez, testified that the governor "became excited to a high degree against all citizens of the United States, and more particularly against me, charging me publicly with having been the cause of the loss of his goods."[4]

Armijo's tantrum, in fact, was wasted. His nephew, having a business head on his shoulders, had taken the precaution of insuring the cargo. Soon after the sinking of the *Lebanon*, he returned to New York with Salazar's relative, collected on his claim, and replaced the shipment. One newspaper editor wrote: "It was certainly fortunate for these men that they lost their goods before reaching Independence; had they lost them upon the road from that place to Santa Fe they might have whistled for the insurance."[5]

The importance of this incident is that it was generally believed that the original Armijo-Salazar money represented funds they had seized from the Texan Santa Fe prisoners. When their agents were once again in Missouri, with replacement for the *Lebanon* loss in hand, the *St. Louis New Era* advised readers that "These merchants . . . are now ready to set out to Santa Fe with the annual caravan of traders from Missouri, and it is not concealed that they will be robbed."[6] The potential robbers, as everyone was now plainly aware, were the Warfield and McDaniel parties. Since at least some of the members of Warfield's unit were thought to have been participants in the Texan Santa Fe Expedition, the *New Orleans Weekly Picayune* opined that they would only be stealing "their own money back."[7]

There is no evidence that John McDaniel seriously considered attacking the spring caravan from Independence. His force would have been too small for that, and in any case the majority of the merchants and teamsters were Americans who could be counted upon to defend the Mexican travelers in their company. That is not to say, however, that once he joined Warfield at Point of Rocks and once the American caravan had crossed the international boundary into Mexico, he might not have been prepared to argue for just such an assault. But the arrival of Chávez on the scene was to push that possibility into the background.

About 1 April, just at the moment Captain McDaniel was leading his men out of Westport, the much reduced party of Don Antonio was nearing Pawnee Rock and the Great Bend of the Arkansas. Ever since the storm on the Cimarron Cutoff, the New Mexicans had been suffering great distress, to such a degree that somewhere in this vicinity Chávez placed a servant on one of the few remaining mules and instructed him to push ahead to Independence and from there to send back assistance. The servant, or "express" as he was referred to at the time, undertook his task faithfully, but at some point along the trail in eastern Kansas he had the ill luck to fall into the clutches of the McDaniel gang.

It is conceivable that the poor man did not at first understand the character of the persons with whom he was dealing and so, innocently, divulged his master's location and the weakness of his condition. One account states that the express was captured and obliged to turn around and lead the gang back to Chávez.[8] That raises the possibility that information was obtained from him by the use of force. Either way, McDaniel now had the intelligence he needed to carry out his act of piracy.

Several accounts of the episode suggest that Antonio José Chávez was stopped and seized sometime between 7 and 10 April as he approached the crossing of the Little Arkansas River, about 240 miles west of Independence. Actually, the encounter seems to have occurred some ten miles west of that point at what was then known as Owl Creek, really a bushy gully that ran south about ten miles, crossed the Santa Fe Trail, and below it emptied into Cow Creek.[9] Regrettably, nothing is known of Chávez's first reaction as he learned that he was suddenly a prisoner. It could have only been a terrifying revelation.

Contemporary versions of what transpired over the next several days agree in general outline, but differ markedly in some of the fine details. Later, when individual gang members were interrogated and then gave testimony in court, their statements, being entirely self-serving, were often in conflict. But a careful sifting of the available data presents the following picture.

Don Antonio and the servants, together with the wagon, were marched several miles down Owl Creek by their roguish-looking captors. At a convenient site John McDaniel called a halt and the party encamped. The next day or so was spent in dividing the spoils, described as "specie, gold bullion and a small lot of furs."[10] The lengthy amount of time involved, for such a simple task, would lead one to believe that the distribution was attended by a good deal of argument. Josiah Gregg declares that each man's share amounted to five hundred dollars.[11] Apparently at no time was there mention of setting aside of one half of the booty for delivery to the Republic of Texas, as per Warfield's original agreement with his sponsors. That in itself clearly establishes the character of Don Antonio's assailants — they were common highway robbers, not the legitimate soldiers of fortune they would later claim to be.

During the interval required for the division of the Chávez property, John McDaniel began to speak of killing the captive. That grim proposal at once produced a split in the ranks. About half the party, led by Dr. Prefontaine and including Berry, the Harris brothers, McCormick, Morton, and Tolbert, objected vigorously.[12] McDaniel made a persuasive argument that should Chávez be released he would doubtless press on to Missouri and acquaint the authorities with the crime and provide enough information to identify those involved. Notwithstanding, members of the opposition, perhaps assailed by conscience for the theft already committed, refused to participate in the monstrous act now being urged by their leader.

It is probably accurate to assume that John McDaniel would have resorted to force against Dr. Prefontaine and the others, but for the strength of their numbers. What happened afterward leads to that conclusion. As it was, he felt obliged to allow their departure. That occurred, it is believed, on the second day after the gang went into camp on Owl Creek. The previous night all the saddle horses and the captured mules had stampeded, leaving the entire company afoot. Since an incident such as that was usually quite avoidable, it strengthens the impression that the enterprise from first to last was attended by monumental ineptitude.

Owing to the loss of their mounts, Dr. Prefontaine and his companions found it necessary to shoulder their plunder, which amounted to considerable weight, and begin walking back toward Missouri. The parting, from all indications, was made under a cloud of bitterness. But once it had occurred, Captain John McDaniel was left free from any challenge to his leadership or his decisions.

The events that shortly unfolded were described in numerous accounts, usually in a straightforward but condensed fashion. Of these, Josiah Gregg's is representative and to the point. After the Prefontaine faction had left, he says: "The other eight cast lots which four should shoot the unfortunate prisoner. It fell upon the two McDaniels, Mason, and one of the Searcy's, but the latter objecting, Brown volunteered in his place: so the ruffians took him out of sight of his men [that is, the servants], beyond a hill, and assassinated him by a number of rifle and pistol shots. The motive for this inhuman act can hardly be divined; for he had been for three days their unresisting prisoner; they feared perhaps he was too resolute to return quietly back to Santa Fe, but would follow them to the settlements and give information."[13]

Statements made by several of the participants at their arrest and still later in court permit Gregg's bare outline to be fleshed out considerably. Perhaps the best recital comes from the testimony of Thomas Towson, described as "simple-minded and honest," who appears to have been an elderly employee of the brothers Searcy.[14] This is his version of the slaying and the circumstances leading up to it.

"Early in the morning of the day when Chavis [sic] was killed, Gallatin Searcy told him that it had been decided that Chavis was that morning to be put out of the way, and that he (Towson) was to be the executioner. He replied to Searcy that he had not joined the expedition to rob and murder peaceful and unoffending men.

"Searcy said that if he would not obey his orders, they would kill him; to which Towson said, he could not believe they would do any such thing; at all events he would not raise his hands against Chavis, let the consequences be what they might. Searcy still persisted in requiring him to undertake the killing, and told him that Brown would be associated with him in the act; but that he positively refused to have anything to do with the matter. Searcy then said they must make some other arrangement.

"Sometime afterwards, on the same morning, McDaniel said in the presence of all the men, that Chavis must be killed, and that lots should be cast, to determine who should do the deed. He (Towson) again refused to have anything to do with the murder; but when McDaniel said that none should refuse to draw lots, with a manner which conveyed to his mind a certainty that his own life would be taken, unless he submitted to the chance proposed, he went forward with a hope that Providence would save him from the commission of so horrible a crime, and was fortunate in drawing a short straw. He also agreed with Mason's [testimony] as to the manner of casting lots, by drawing straws, and to the persons who were thus detailed. He also corroborated Mason's statement, that one of the Searcy's drew a long straw, and making some objection to the service, Brown volunteered as his substitute.

"Towson also stated that McDaniel took Chavis out from the camp, apparently to have some conversation with him, and was followed by David McDaniel, Mason and Brown, close in the rear; that he saw them go out and steadily kept his eye upon them the whole time; that when about fifty yards from the camp, he saw John McDaniel present his pistol against Chavis and fire. Chavis immediately sprang off, and ran with his best speed. The other men fired, but Chavis continued to run for nearly one hundred yards, pursued by John McDaniel, who came nearly up to him and again fired, and then ran up and pushed or tripped Chavis, so that he fell. Brown came up next, but did not fire; — Mason next arrived and fired, which was the last shot fired."[15]

This story was virtually identical with that of William Mason who turned state's evidence against his accomplices. According to a press report: "The only difference in the statement made by Towson and the testimony of Mason, is as to the distance run by Chavis after receiving McDaniel's first shot; that Chavis threw up his arms and ran forward a few yards, and that he and all the others fired immediately, and Chavis fell dead."[16]

At the time of his arrest, Mason made one other illuminating remark. He claimed that while it was true he had fired at Chávez, he had not done so until after he was dead, and then only through fear, believing McDaniel would shoot him if he refused.[17] It is impossible to establish the veracity of Mason's assertion, of course, but it appears to have a ring of authenticity. John McDaniel clearly stands as the villain in the piece, and except for Joseph Brown who eagerly followed his lead, the others all look to be reluctant partners in homicide. That even includes David McDaniel, a seemingly timorous youth completely under the malignant influence of his older brother.

Another small detail about the murder that also cannot be confirmed is this: stray reports suggest that in the last moments some conversation passed between McDaniel and Chávez, when the latter begged for his life. Although eyewitnesses neglected to mention the matter, it certainly remains plausible.[18]

After the slaying, Chávez's body was searched and he was found to have been wearing a money belt. It produced, by McDaniel's own admission, thirty-nine gold doubloons.[19] That discovery prompted a more thorough examination of the wagon and its contents. Says Gregg, "The banditti now ransacked and rifled everything, and found about $3,000 worth of gold dust in a trunk."[20] On the first day the men had broken into the locked jockey box attached to the outside of the wagon. That had yielded the bulk of the loot and, as noted, had been distributed among the entire gang. But the new finds — the doubloons and the dust hidden, perhaps in a secret compartment, in the trunk — had to be shared by only half the number, since Dr. Prefontaine's group withdrew the day before.

In his *Commerce of the Prairies*, published just one year after the murder, Gregg informs us that "The body of the unfortunate man, together with his wagon and baggage, were thrown into a neighboring ravine."[21] Elsewhere, he states they were thrown into a creek.[22] His meaning is the same in both cases, for it is known that the corpse was tossed unceremoniously into the deep gully of Owl Creek where it was left exposed to the elements and predators.

Only one thing remained unattended to, and that was the disposition of Don Antonio's retainers. Their servile manner must have convinced John McDaniel that there was no chance they would attempt to continue eastward. So, after a thorough search to be sure they had no bit of their master's treasure secreted about their persons, they were turned loose and told to return to Santa Fe. Setting them adrift on the plains unarmed, dismounted, without supplies, and in a season when the weather could still turn harsh was practically a death sentence in itself. If they did not perish from hunger or exposure in the more than three hundred miles to Bent's Fort, the first place on the New Mexico border where relief could be obtained, then it was likely they would fall victim to a war party of Indians out on its first raid of the spring. Presumably, McDaniel was counting on one of those eventualities to eliminate the witnesses.

After the servants were banished from the camp on Owl Creek, members of the diminished gang, now with blood on their hands, made preparations to leave. Those remaining, to recapitulate, were the McDaniels, Joseph Brown and William Mason — the foursome who carried out the murder — and, Thomas Towson, Schuyler Oldham, and Gallatin and Christopher Searcy. Just as they were on the verge of taking the trail, eight or ten of their horses that had stampeded two nights before were found. That allowed every man a mount with a spare or two left over to serve as pack animals for the gold, silver, and bales of furs.

There are some indications that McDaniel may have actually guided the slim party on toward the rendezvous with Warfield, but a few days afterward, perhaps in the neighborhood of the Great Bend, he abandoned the plan and wheeled about, apparently because of hostile Indian sign. Whether that occurred, or whether the turnaround took place at once on Owl Creek, the fact is the men were soon pointed eastward up the Santa Fe Trail in the direction of Missouri. As yet John McDaniel had no inkling of the tempest his vicious little escapade had set loose. It may have been, as Uncle Dick Wootton wrote later, that he thought, being so far beyond the pale of the law, he could commit any sort of crime with impunity. Indeed, McDaniel might have gotten away with it, reckoned Uncle Dick, but for the fact that Chávez was a man of so much importance, his death brought a swift and exacting punishment.[23]

CHAPTER

IV

THE CHASE

THE GENTRYS were of a prolific pioneer family, a number of whom migrated from Kentucky around the time of the War of 1812 and settled in the Boone's Lick country of central Missouri. After the Santa Fe Trail was opened in 1821, several of them left farming and became heavily involved in commerce with New Mexico and the north Mexican provinces. Two members of the clan so engaged, cousins Nicholas and Reuben Gentry, by chance came to play a role in the pursuit and capture of the Chávez slayers.[1]

Nicholas was trading in Santa Fe by 1825, as indicated by an invoice in the Mexican customs records, which also shows him as a resident of Columbia, Missouri.[2] He would remain active on the trail for the next thirty years, sometimes as an independent merchant but other times as a guide or wagonmaster in the employ of others. His fellow traders and the Mexican authorities at Santa Fe referred to him as "Old Contraband Gentry," because of his adeptness at smuggling goods past customs officials. Governor Manuel Armijo was said to have tolerated his lapse of honesty because he always gambled away his profits and thus took nothing out of the country.[3] John C. McCoy of Westport, well acquainted with Nicholas, described him as "an odd genius, full of dry humor who made others laugh while he remained solemn as a poet."[4]

Reuben Gentry made his initial trip to New Mexico in 1832 at age sixteen, working as a teamster. By 1839 he went as the wagonmaster, or supercargo, for a thirty-schooner caravan owned by the firm of Giddings and Patterson. The train paused in Santa Fe only long enough to go through customs, then it proceeded down the Rio Grande and across the desert to Chihuahua where the freight was sold. The following year, Reuben formed a partnership with James M. Giddings and opened a store in Santa Fe. He was there in 1841 during the furor created by the appearance of the Texan Santa Fe Expedition and was among thirteen resident American merchants who wrote Secretary of State Daniel Webster expressing fear they would be harmed by Mexican officials in retaliation for the invasion from Texas.[5]

The political climate soon improved, allowing Reuben to leave Santa Fe and transfer his interests to Chihuahua where he spent the next two years in merchandising. Then in March 1843, he was engaged as a wagonmaster by a British firm doing business in the Mexican city of Zacatecas. His instructions were to go overland to Independence and there take charge of twelve wagon loads of English goods, shipped under bond to that point, and transport them back along the Santa Fe and Chihuahua trails to Zacatecas. Later that month Reuben reached Santa Fe where he learned of the departure a short time before of Antonio José Chávez. He was also informed that the annual westbound caravan would leave for the States about 1 April and, no doubt, he was advised, for safety reasons, to wait and accompany it. However, unwilling to brook so long a delay, and knowing that a large train would travel slowly, he set out on the trail at once with a slender party of three companions.[6]

Gentry and his men rode hard and made good time, gradually gaining on Chávez. It is possible that they may have encountered some of Don Antonio's deserting servants and learned of his strained circumstances. Beyond the Great Bend in central Kansas, Gentry came upon the last campfire of the Mexicans beside the trail. So close was he that he expected to overtake and join them on the next day. Instead, much to his surprise, he observed that in the vicinity of Owl Creek Don Antonio's wagon tracks left the road and turned south. He assumed at first that the trader had veered off a short distance seeking a better way and he still expected to meet him up ahead when he rejoined the main route. But as time passed and neither Chávez nor his wagon appeared, Reuben Gentry became increasingly uneasy. Finally, he concluded that the man had met with foul play, but his own company being so weak he dismissed any thought of returning to search for him. So he hurried on to Independence to spread the alarm, reaching there on 19 April.[7]

Even before Gentry arrived on the border with his startling news, belated steps had been taken to thwart the McDaniel gang as well as the rumored Warfield Expedition. It will be recalled that in mid-March worried residents of Independence had dispatched a letter to the Indian superintendent in St. Louis with tidings of McDaniel's plans. They may have also approached the local Indian Agent R. W. Cummins for it is known that on 1 April he sent an urgent appeal to Colonel Richard B. Mason, commander at Fort Leavenworth, thirty miles up the Missouri, asking for military assistance. Three days later sixty members of the First Dragoons left the fort in pursuit of McDaniel's marauders. Evidently their intention was to arrest them for lacking proper passports, as no offense beyond that was suspected.[8] Gregg claims the soldiers followed the trail just over one hundred miles before giving up and returning, which would seem about right since it is recorded that they carried only seven days' rations.[9] However, other reports state that the Dragoons penetrated much deeper into Kansas. The editor of the *St. Louis New Era*, for example, afterward blamed Colonel Mason for failure to protect the murdered Chávez, saying that had the troops "kept on one day longer, they would have reached the place where the attack was made."[10]

The tumult on the frontier prompted additional action on the part of Colonel Stephen Watts Kearny, commander of the army's Third Military Department, whose headquarters were at Jefferson Barracks near St. Louis. Kearny had formerly been stationed at Fort Leavenworth, so he was well versed in matters pertaining to the Santa Fe Trail. On 10 April, that is, a week and a half before Gentry brought word of the Chávez crime to the settlements, the colonel issued an order directing two companies of dragoons from Fort Leavenworth and another company from Fort Scott (located eight miles west of the Missouri border) to rendezvous at Westport one month hence, 10 May. There they were to "be prepared and held in readiness to march to the boundary line between the United States and New Mexico, on the route to Santa Fe, as an escort, for the protection of any and all persons . . . engaged in lawful trade and intercourse between the two countries."[11] In other words, the troops were to usher the annual spring caravan as far as the edge of United States territory as a safeguard against Texan raiders, although the order made no explicit reference to Texas.

Kearny actually had something larger in mind. He wanted the dragoons to continue with the wagons all the way to Santa Fe, or at least until they encountered a patrol of Mexican troops reputed to be serving trail duty. For American forces to cross into Mexico, however, posed a delicate problem of diplomacy. As the editor of the *Missouri Republican* remarked in his paper, while it would be highly improper for the United States to take that action without permission, Mexico should perceive no impropriety or danger in granting it.[12] That was Colonel Kearny's view as well, for he had already written to Secretary of War James M. Porter asking him to obtain permission from the Mexican minister to Washington, Juan N. Almonte, that would allow the American escort to enter and operate in New Mexico.[13]

Minister Almonte was already fully aware of the threat that loomed over traffic on the Santa Fe Trail. The previous fall he had received information from the Mexican consul in New Orleans that Charles Warfield, claiming a Texas commission, was recruiting men for a proposed incursion along the Arkansas River.[14] Either then or early in 1843 Almonte put in his own request for American troops to escort the traders up to the international boundary.[15] But that was as far as he was willing to go. Having served in 1836 as an officer under General Antonio López de Santa Anna at the fall of the Alamo, he was familiar with Texans and their combative ways. Also, his experience in Washington convinced him that any American proposal to enter Mexican lands, even for the innocent purpose of escort duty on the Santa Fe Trail, should be resisted. That conclusion, he felt certain, would be concurred in by his government. Therefore, when Secretary of War Porter approached him with Colonel Kearny's appeal for permission to cross the Arkansas into Mexico, the minister returned a blunt refusal. As a result, instructions were issued to Kearny prohibiting his men under any circumstances from violating the Mexican boundary.[16]

This was the situation, as far as the military was concerned, when Reuben Gentry, forty days from Santa Fe, suddenly appeared in Independence with his disturbing revelation. The very next day, 20 April, the first press report was issued announcing that the trader Chávez had vanished from the trail in the vicinity of the Little Arkansas Crossing. Since McDaniel and perhaps even Warfield were thought to be in that area, it was supposed that the worst had befallen the Mexican and he would never reach Independence.[17] These disclosures spread like a prairie fire to the towns and river landings surrounding the head of the Santa Fe Trail, and according to all available accounts, threw the entire frontier population into the state of greatest excitement and indignation.

Immediately posses were formed, some with official sanction and others without, to reconnoiter the countryside for evidence of Chávez's fate. One party, it has been claimed, was organized at Yoacham's Tavern in Westport with Daniel Yoacham as leader.[18] That now must be regarded as an error, since as will be demonstrated shortly Yoacham was subsequently arrested as an accomplice of the wanted men. If a posse did assemble at the tavern, it was probably the one under charge of the sheriff of Jackson County, George W. Buchanan.[19]

At Independence, as soon as Reuben Gentry's news became known, a company of twenty citizens gathered under the command of William Gilpin and rode west, intending to go all the way to the Little Arkansas. Gilpin, of Quaker background from Pennsylvania, had been tutored in his youth by Nathaniel Hawthorne and briefly attended West Point. Settling in Independence in 1841, he quickly won a name in local affairs. His leadership abilities, already apparent, would lead him to the governorship of the Colorado Territory in 1861.[20]

Gilpin's posse must have been the one that Gregg says found "Chávez's wagon and baggage all torn to pieces, 4 or 5 miles south of the road opposite the point where Gentry last saw the trail. So, it seems at the very time Gentry passed, the banditti were robbing Chávez."[21] According to Gregg, the party could discover no corpse and so knew only that a robbery had been committed. However, Gilpin years later would declare that Chávez's hair had been found, "wolves having reached the body before the posse did."[22] He also added that he had continued with his men along the Santa Fe Trail as far as the later site of Dodge City which was near Warfield's announced rendezvous at Point of Rocks. But finding no trace of Texans or bandits, he returned to Missouri after an absence of two weeks. There he learned that in the interval some of the culprits had been captured.

What had happened to the gang following their crime on Owl Creek? Dr. Prefontaine's faction, which had left first, walked east as far as Council Grove, but finding it increasingly difficult to carry the heavy gold and silver, they cached it thereabouts. Then, splitting up, they proceded on toward the border with the aim of slipping undetected into the settlements, securing horses, and returning for their treasure.

McDaniel's group, having recovered some of its horses, had an easier time of it. But these men, too, as they approached the frontier line broke into several groups, hoping to enter unnoticed. Among the first to come in were the Searcy brothers who boarded the steamer *Weston* at Westport Landing. They rode upriver about a dozen miles to Park's Landing, near present Parkville, Missouri, and there disembarked. From that point they faded into the backwoods communities and were not heard of again.[23]

By a strange coincidence, Reuben Gentry was on the *Weston* at the same time as the Searcys, but failed to recognize them. Apparently, a day or so after his arrival in Independence, he booked passage for Fort Leavenworth, his purpose, we can assume, to give a firsthand report to the military authorities regarding the Chávez affair. On 24 April he was returning on the same steamer when it pulled to the bank near the mouth of the Kansas River, within the present boundaries of Kansas City. Three rough-looking men came on board bearing heavy packs and two bundles of furs.

Gentry took one look at the new passengers and instantly his suspicions were aroused. When they had signed on, he went to the clerk, J. H. Pim, and asked to see the boat's register. In it he observed that the leader of the trio had written, "John McDaniel for Texas." His two companions were listed as David McDaniel and William Mason, and their destination was given as St. Louis. By now, of course, Reuben Gentry was fully informed of the identity of the trail marauders, and he must have been astonished at the stroke of chance that caused his path to cross theirs. His timely discovery was to set off a singular series of events that would end more than a year later at the hangman's gallows.

As the *Weston* paddled slowly down the Missouri, Gentry watched the three passengers, bided his time, and formed a plan. When the steamer docked briefly at Independence Landing, on the south side of the river, he quickly went ashore and delivered a written message to a rider with instructions to carry it to Independence, two and one-half miles away.

The message bore the news that three of the wanted men were on board the *Weston* and that a posse should intercept the boat at Owens Landing. That stop was fifteen miles downstream by water, owing to a sweeping bend in the river, but only six miles overland from Independence. As soon as this word reached Independence Square, a body of twenty armed men immediately made a dash for Owens Landing. They arrived just in time to catch the *Weston*.

The two McDaniel brothers were gone, however. From the point Gentry had dispatched his appeal, the boat had crossed to the north shore of the river to touch at Liberty before proceeding on to Owens Landing. The McDaniels, bound for St. Louis, had not thought to get off there, even though it was their hometown. But they had gotten wind that their secret was out and fearing apprehension if they remained, they left the craft and in the bargain left their traveling companion, William Mason. As already noted, Mason was afraid of John McDaniel and would later claim at the trial that he fired at Chávez only because he believed his own life to be in danger. Thus, it is clear that there was no loyalty among these thieves, which explains why the McDaniels so readily deserted Mason, without any hint of a warning about the danger they suspected ahead.

No sooner had the *Weston* tied up at Owens Landing than members of the posse from Independence rushed on board and made a thorough search of the boat. William Mason, probably pointed out by Gentry and clerk Pim, was immediately arrested and taken on shore. With him were seized the two bundles of beaver fur that had been looted from Chávez's wagon. A witness reported seeing Mason drop something overboard just before he was taken, and investigation of the water soon brought up nine Mexican doubloons. In addition, some counterfeit bank paper was found on his person. All of this was strong evidence that he was a party to crime.

After a few minutes of intense interrogation there on the landing, Mason confessed all, describing the murder, the events leading up to it, and revealing the identities of each of the gang members. His was the first confirmation of the death of Chávez, for the return of Gilpin's posse from the trail was still more than a week away. Within a few days the grim details he now disclosed would be widely circulated in the press. John McDaniel had committed a serious error in allowing his accomplice to fall into the hands of the law.

While the prisoner Mason was sent to Independence under guard, the Jackson County posse turned its attention to the two men who had eluded their grasp by escaping to Liberty. The Missouri was at flood stage and the ferries that normally provided transportation across the river to Clay County were in dock, unable to navigate. The *Weston*, as a large paddlewheeler, however, could manage the full current with no trouble. In the emergency the boat's master, Mr. Littlejohn, agreed to break his schedule by taking on eight or ten members of the posse and their horses and carrying them to a bluff rising above the flood waters on the other side. From that location, it was but a ride of a few miles on high ground to Liberty. Later it would be learned that John McDaniel, with the ferries out, thought himself "secure beyond the turbid stream." It never occurred to him that the *Weston* might be pressed into use by a posse.[24]

It is perhaps of passing interest to observe that, after depositing the Jackson men and their mounts on the north bank, the *Weston* continued its downriver passage, arriving at St. Louis late at night on 28 April. The story of the eventful trip, plus the first report of the Chávez murder and confession of Mason, were related by "the gentlemanly clerk Mr. Pim" and the details were accorded prominent place in the local press.[25] For the *Weston*, which had been in service only a short time, its part in the Chávez case was to prove its sole claim to a tiny footnote in history. Not long afterward, the steamer burned to its waterline near St. Charles.[26]

At Liberty meanwhile, events had moved rapidly. Three or four days before the brothers McDaniel arrived on the *Weston*, another of the original gang, Samuel O. Berry, who had been part of Dr. Prefontaine's group, reached town. To those citizens who were acquainted with the intent of the enterprise, he announced that the McDaniel company had been unable to join Warfield and that the expedition turned back, a complete failure. Owing to the flood and the disruption of communication with towns below the river, it was several days before information was received that disputed his story.

The facts of the matter were introduced by members of the Jackson County posse who rode into Liberty and proclaimed their errand. Without delay they were advised that John McDaniel was then at the office of the Clay County clerk, Abraham Shaffer. Going to that office, they seized McDaniel just inside the door and disarmed him. Also present were Shaffer and a Judge Thompson. As McDaniel was led away, they left the office and Shaffer locked his door behind him.[27]

One report of the incident declares that upon seeing the approach of the posse, John McDaniel made a show of resistance and attempted to draw his pistol. But he was overpowered before he could accomplish his purpose. He was afterward heard to remark that those who apprehended him were fortunate in preventing his laying a hand on the gun, for had he succeeded, he would certainly have shot one of them.[28]

Inexplicably, it would appear that the smooth talking McDaniel rather quickly managed to convince his captors that they had made a mistake. That is the only conclusion that can readily be drawn from a statement made by Clerk Shaffer: "It is known that on the day [26 April] John McDaniel made his appearance in Liberty, and in less than an hour afterwards was seized by some citizens of Jackson upon a charge of murder. A short time after he was released, but, having attempted to escape, was pursued, re-taken, and delivered to the custody of his pursuers."[29] Younger brother David and Samuel O. Berry were also summarily nabbed.

Abraham Shaffer now fell under suspicion. As the *Missouri Republican* subsequently described the circumstances: "The plunder of the two McDaniels was found concealed in the office of the clerk of the court of Clay County, who is suspected of being a party in the affair, and his conduct would warrant such belief. He refused, while citizens were searching the premises, to open a drawer in his secretary, allowing as the reason that it contained private papers, but dreading the anger of the mob about his office, he submitted, and upon examination, the drawer was found to contain $1,500 of the plunder. This fact, in our opinion, would warrant his arrest as an accomplice — indeed, it is generally believed that he furnished the McDaniels with the means for their outfit."[30]

The accusation proved so serious and the evidence appeared so damaging that in an effort to defend himself Shaffer on 1 May had printed at his own expense a broadside for public distribution. Its purpose was to counter "all the various and contradictory stories afloat" concerning his relationship with the McDaniels and in a "candid" manner set the record straight. This document, arranged in two columns of type, represents the most detailed recital of events surrounding the capture of the culprits that has thus far come to light.

In the broadside Shaffer says that about an hour after the arrest of John McDaniel he was called back to his office by sundry leading citizens, among them Judge Thompson and Sheriff Baxter. Arriving there he discovered a large crowd outside crying for him to unlock the door. He stoutly refused to admit the unruly throng, but did agree to enter with several gentlemen and the sheriff. Apparently McDaniel had confessed to leaving some of his possessions with the clerk and Sheriff Baxter now ordered that these be produced. The press version of what followed, as already noted, is that Shaffer refused to open a secretary drawer, claiming that it contained private papers, and that he only relented through fear of the mob out front.

Shaffer's rebuttal, understandably, places a different and less prejudicial color on the matter. He affirms: "My hesitation for a few moments in giving those gentlemen the key of the wardrobe [what the paper called a secretary] where McDaniel had deposited his effects, the character of which I knew not, for I had not thought of examining them, will be censured by my friends, and readily seized hold of by my enemies for the purpose of doing me serious injury. This, I admit, was imprudent on my part and an error of judgment; I am nevertheless unconscious that any moral guilt attaches to me in the affair, however my motives may be misconstrued."

But there were other matters that lent his actions an unfavorable odor, at least in the eyes of his neighbors. After the sheriff and the mob departed, Shaffer had made a further search of his wardrobe and found a large amount of gold dust and bullion that had been missed. It was said against him that he had delayed until the next day in turning the new discovery over to the authorities, though Shaffer denied it. He was also censured for receiving John McDaniel in his office upon his return from the trail.

The clerk responded that the last charge was utterly frivolous because up to that time the accused had been regarded by everyone as a respectable citizen. Moreover, since Berry had spread the tale that the expedition was a failure, there was then no reason to suspect McDaniel of criminal activity. And he added: "I am fully persuaded that to impartial men many reasons will readily occur why I should not have expelled a young man from my office with whom I had been acquainted for many years, before I knew that he had committed any offense against the laws of the country."

That Shaffer was a long time friend of McDaniel will explain why he had lent him fifty dollars before the expedition's depature. It was that perhaps innocent act of friendship that would lead the *Missouri Republican* to charge that he had furnished the gang "with the means for their outfit." In reply, the clerk stated that because of his loan to McDaniel, "it is contended that I was to share in the profits of his rash and criminal act, and that his object in returning direct to this town was to make the division of the Chávez spoils with me." That was absurd, he pointed out, because as was now well known, the McDaniel brothers had bought passage on the *Weston* for St. Louis and only got off at Liberty owing to their fear of capture at Owens Landing.

"John McDaniel always disavowed to me, and I presume to every other citizen," continued Shaffer, "the intention of committing any act of hostility against Mexicans or any other persons within the territory of the U. States, nor did I ever suppose he would be guilty of an act of this description. In the expedition itself, whatever may have been its object, I had no interest, and expected nothing from it." The fifty-dollar loan, plus an older debt of one hundred fifty dollars had been secured by John McDaniel with a promissory note against the will of his father William McDaniel. That was how he expected to be repaid, claimed Shaffer, not from John's "proceeds of his Lilliputian warfare upon Mexico."[31]

All of Abraham Shaffer's answers, directed toward his own vindication, seem perfectly plausible and, indeed, he appears to have been the victim of circumstances. Notwithstanding, in the charged atmosphere following upon the heels of the murder, his fellow townspeople were clearly prepared to believe the worst. Their suspicions seemed confirmed when the clerk was indicted as an accessory the following September.[32]

Following their arrest in Liberty, the McDaniels and Berry were taken to Independence and lodged in jail. The total amount of booty recovered with them is given as thirty-six hundred dollars in gold dust, silver bullion, and doubloons.[33] Once behind bars, Berry made a full confession which was added to that already volunteered by Mason. Because he had been seized with the McDaniels, the earliest press reports mistakenly identified Berry as one of the gang's ringleaders.[34]

Once the details of the Chávez slaying became known, efforts were redoubled to apprehend those still at large by closing all avenues of escape. The men of Jackson and Clay counties assembled new posses and commenced scouring the country around the head of the Santa Fe Trail. Parties rode all night to intercept boats on the Missouri River and place guards at the principal landings.[35] The next to be taken was Joseph Brown, he who had voluntarily replaced one of the Searcys as an executioner. Brown had gotten as far as Camden, a river town about twenty miles east of Liberty. There on 29 April he sold his horse and bought a ticket on the steamer *Ione*. The boat had just pulled away when a posse reached the landing, but it promptly returned and delivered the fugitive into custody. He was found to be carrying five hundred dollars in silver.[36]

In his confession Samuel Berry divulged that the Prefontaine group had buried its share of the Chávez loot near Council Grove. As soon as that became known another posse of ten men was collected under the leadership of Nicholas Gentry to go and attempt to retrieve it. "Old Nick" must have been active during the entire episode, as indicated by a hotel bill from the Noland House on Independence Square which shows that he was charged $5.38, "To board while on pursuit of McDaniel and others."[37]

Gentry's posse had advanced along the trail about one hundred miles when Dr. Prefontaine and another man unexpectedly fell into their hands. The doctor had gone back to the cache and was returning with twenty-six hundred dollars in silver coin. His companion was none other than the tavern keeper from Westport, Daniel Yoacham! The pair were speedily placed under arrest and conducted to Independence. But there Yoacham "was set at liberty, upon the ground that he was not *fully* advised of the crime they had committed."[38] The degree of his complicity in the entire McDaniel business stands as a mystery to this day.

It is plain that Dr. Prefontaine, bearing witness to the dictum that no honor exists among thieves, was collared in the process of making off with the treasure belonging to his fellow marauders. That assumption is borne out by the fact that two of them, William Harris and Nathaniel Morton, likewise went out independently to recover the buried coin. They were accompanied by Edward Peyton of Cass County, Missouri, the depth of whose involvement, like that of Yoacham, remains murky.[39]

Still another posse pursued them and caught all three on the open prairie about halfway to Council Grove. As that party was coming back, Josiah Gregg informs us that "it met with old Tommy Towson amongst the Potawatamie Indians, who showed no inclination to escape. Poor old fellow! He is surely to be pitied. He seems of innocent character, but is very simple; and was beguiled into the scrape by the Searcys who took him upon hire; and thus being in their employ, he was forced to remain and witness the murder. But he showed so much dissatisfaction, and simplicity withal, that, as it appeared evident from the confessions, John McD. the captain of the band, had determined to have him killed, lest he should disclose upon them when they reached the settlements: but the old man getting wind of it, made his escape one night, without money or provisions, perhaps 150 miles from the settlements; and but for the fortune of falling in with some friendly Indians, must have perished. It is to be hoped that he will be acquitted."[40]

Gregg adds that with the latest arrests, plus that of John McCormick, for a total of ten of the original gang, the amount of Chávez's property recovered came to more than seven thousand dollars. "It was first believed that Chávez had from $30 to $32,000; it has since been ascertained that he was bringing in but $10 or $11,000."[41] The loot still missing was in the hands of those five who had managed to elude capture: the Searcys and Schuyler Oldham were thought to have fled eastward toward the Mississippi, while Benjamin Harris and Benjamin F. Tolbert escaped down the Missouri in a canoe.

From St. Louis, the *Missouri Republican*, which had been following the case closely and apprising readers of developments, issued a word of congratulations: "Much praise is due the citizens of Jackson and Clay counties for the promptness which they have displayed in arresting so daring a band."[42] While true that only two-thirds of the gang were in jail at Independence, among their number were the four guilty of actually shooting Don Antonio José Chávez. All that remained to be done was for the wheels of justice to grind out judgments upon the accused. But even on the Missouri frontier, where such matters were customarily handled with celerity, another year would pass before the final chapter was written.

CHAPTER

V

THE TRIAL

ON 20 APRIL 1843 Josiah Gregg reached his parents' farm four miles northeast of Independence, close to Owens Landing. Returning from a trip to Arkansas, he carried with him a portion of the manuscript that would be published the following year under the title *Commerce of the Prairies* and that would earn him a secure place in the annals of the Santa Fe Trail. In those days immediately after his arrival, Gregg found that the local population was much astir over two events — the flood on the Missouri River and the murder of Antonio José Chávez. The second matter soon assumed precedence in public attention as members of the McDaniel gang were brought in piecemeal by the posses and deposited in the Independence jail.

It is said that Gregg visited the prisoners in the lock-up, which very well may be true, since he was known for his natural inquisitiveness, supported by a habit of writing down in a journal "everything he deemed worthy of remembrance."[1] Quite likely he was personally acquainted with some of the accused, for this far part of Missouri was still thinly settled and people regarded residents of adjacent towns as neighbors. By his own statement, Gregg is known to have discussed the details of the case with Reuben Gentry and other prominent Santa Fe traders who had participated in the capture of the gang. Being a merchant himself, having first gone to New Mexico in 1831, he enjoyed an easy familiarity with the trading fraternity and was thus in a position to collect the facts of the episode as they were then known.[2] His published version, appearing afterward in the *Arkansas Intelligencer* and, in abbreviated form, in *Commerce of the Prairies*, was the one most often quoted by later writers.[3]

For a while some hope was entertained that the five outlaws remaining on the loose would yet be apprehended and a reward of five hundred dollars each was posted for their delivery. Meanwhile, a few days after their arrest John and David McDaniel were sent down the Missouri on the steamer *Oceana* to St. Louis, arriving 2 May. They were escorted by several deputized citizens of Jackson County who took the opportunity to bring newspapers in that city up to date on developments.[4] Back in Independence, Dr. Prefontaine, brought in from the prairies after departure of the McDaniels, was subjected to interrogation and then he and the rest of the gang were also dispatched to St. Louis.

An interesting commentary on these events is provided by the great naturalist John James Audubon who in the spring of 1843 was making his last expedition west, going by steamer to the upper Missouri. Stopping at Independence he heard from a friend the "news respecting the murder of Mr. Jarvis." He was told that twenty picked men of the neighborhood [the Gilpin posse] were still in pursuit of "the rascally thieves and murderers." And to that, Audubon wrote in his journal: "I hope they will overtake them all and shoot them on the spot."[5] As to the McDaniel brothers, already under arrest, he said in a letter: "The rascals that Shot and plundered him [Chávez] are now under way to St. Louis on their trial, and if not *pardoned* must be hanged. — I wish I was in the Jury, I would have both and all of them Shot at the door of the Court House as soon as the verdict of Willful Murder is past against them. Strange to say those very men Stood in their own portion of the country as Men Honourable and of good Standing. So much for the love of plunder and Money."[6]

The murder and robbery of Don Antonio, occurring in the unorganized territory beyond the states, fell under the federal jurisdiction of the U.S. Circuit Court for the District of Missouri. It was for that reason the offenders were conducted to St. Louis for their initial arraignment.[7] Later the question of jurisdiction would play a significant role in the appeal process.[8]

The McDaniel brothers were no more off the steamer from Independence than the formal proceedings against them got under way.

On 3 May Circuit Court Judge John Catron, who was also an associate justice of the U.S. Supreme Court, granted a motion to summon a special time for the holding of a trial for the Chávez murders.

A press notice of that date announced that, "The court will sit as soon as witnesses can be summoned (some of them from Santa Fe) for this purpose."[9] By the third week in May all ten of the gang who had been arrested were incarcerated in St. Louis. It was reported that Dr. Prefontaine "looks well and betrays no serious concern about the scrape he has got into. In fact they all entertain but little apprehension of the result of their coming trial."[10] Their confidence evidently resided in a misplaced belief that their crime against Chávez could be satisfactorily explained away.

The case, so widely publicized and commented upon by the press, reflected the strong concern in that era for moral issues. An elaborately justified code of conduct, in which ideas of right and wrong were firmly fixed by law and community consensus, served as the basis for social order. But within the framework of the code considerable room existed for discussion of both theoretical points and practical considerations. In that context, men of the Missouri border debated the actions of John McDaniel and his accomplices.

Given the common notion that frontier society was lawless and unsafe, the degree of probity that actually prevailed in the Santa Fe trade appears remarkable. Shippers routinely stored crates and hogsheads of merchandise, unguarded and covered only by canvas, on the river landings for days at a time before they were loaded on New Mexico-bound freight wagons. Theft of such exposed goods was unheard of. José Chávez, brother of the slain Don Antonio, is reputed to have once left rawhide bags containing one hundred thousand dollars in Mexican silver overnight on the sidewalk in front of a Westport store where he planned to conduct business the following morning.[11] William R. Bernard, a leading Missouri outfitter, remarked: "The traders and trappers of the period were an exceedingly honest body of men. It seemed not to occur to them to do otherwise than pay their debts when it was possible for them to do so. Almost the whole of this business was done upon a credit of from six to twelve months."[12] Where such strict attitudes of conduct prevailed, it is not surprising that the overwhelming sentiment of the day toward the McDaniel gang was one of anger and revulsion, and others, besides Audubon, were quick to demand capital punishment for those charged with the Chávez killing.

Notwithstanding, there were some who were willing to listen to a defense based on the claim that the murder was not a murder, but a legitimate reprisal visited by Texas upon its sworn enemy, Mexico. Given the body of evidence against them, gang members freely admitted their participation in the crime, but "justifying it under a commission given one of them [John McDaniel] as a captain in Texas."[13]

In response to this ingenuous excuse one St. Louis journalist hastened to editorialize: "A strange hallucination seems to have taken possession of a portion of the public mind upon this subject. It is argued, that because Capt. McDaniel had a Texan commission in his pocket — real or forged, and Mexico and Texas entertained a hostile attitude toward each other, — that, therefore, the unfortunate Charvis, he being a Mexican, was a fit subject for murder by a band of robbers, and no punishment ought, or can be inflicted upon them for this cruel act. We do not suppose that this argument obtains with any numerous class, but we notice it to say, that Charvis was on American territory; that he was as much entitled to the protection of our laws as the president of the United States himself; that the law being violated, knows not distinction, or ought to know none, in citizenship, color, or station in life; that the acts of plunder and murder in this case deserve the severest punishment in the penitentiary, and on the gallows; and that no Texian commission, nothing in the past life . . . of these banditti, or in the relations of Texas and Mexico to each other, ought to weigh a feather in preventing the execution of the law upon them."[14]

Almost at once efforts were made to disassociate McDaniel and his men from Colonel Warfield. One of the first press announcements, for example, proclaimed: "These men were acting on their 'own account' and had not joined Warfield when the attack upon the Mexicans was made."[15] The *New Orleans Weekly Picayune*, a fiercely pro-Texan paper, held Warfield blameless for the murder, since he had no direct hand in it. "In saying this," noted the editor, "we are far from justifying the killing of Chavis, of whose death Warfield is perfectly innocent according to all accounts."[16] At least one Texas newspaper, while recognizing the odious nature of the crime, joined the chorus in defense of Warfield. The *Galveston Civilian* informed readers: "There is no reason to believe that this murder was either expected or authorized by Col. Warfield, and we regard him as no more responsible for it than if it had been committed by Indians or other persons whom he had never seen."[17] Plainly, the writer was unaware that John McDaniel had been personally recruited by Warfield.

Behind the public expressions of support for Colonel Warfield, of course, lay the hope, in some quarters at least, that the Republic of Texas might be cleared of involvement in the Chávez homicide. That could best be done by repudiating John McDaniel and demonstrating that his gang acted entirely independently of the Warfield Expedition. Further muddying the waters for the Republic was the assumption made by some people, unfamiliar with the finer details of the case, that McDaniel and company were, in fact, residents of Texas. That mistake is still made by a few careless writers today. Rufus Sage, one of the men enlisted in the Rockies by Warfield after he left Missouri, went to great pains in his memoirs to point out emphatically that "the murderers of Charvis *were not* Texans."[18] [Emphasis his.]

Inevitably perhaps, the fallout could not be deflected from the shoulders of Warfield. The St. Louis press issued a call for his arrest and urged President Houston of Texas to "disavow having commissioned him for the business in which he has been engaged."[19] Subsequently, the Republic moved to do just that; however, its action was taken not because of the Chávez affair, but rather in answer to an earlier protest from the United States over Warfield's recruiting activities on American soil. Isaac Van Zandt, the Texas representative in Washington, advised the secretary of state on 4 August 1843 that "Texas disclaims giving its sanction to any act of Colonel Warfield which should violate the rights or hazard the neutral obligations or relations of the United States; and that a letter, revoking the powers of Colonel Warfield, has been dispatched to him."[20] Since no Texas official had the slightest idea of the whereabouts of the colonel, it is doubtful whether any letter reached him.

The debate over the Chávez episode, to the degree that there was one, tended to be colored by American attitudes toward Mexicans and Mexico. A New York newspaper, remarking upon the murder, explained that it could well have been anticipated since for years lawless elements from Missouri had "made immense sums of money . . . mule stealing from the Santa Fe Mexicans and Indians." And the paper added, "It is no crime with them, to rob and kill a Mexican, or to shoot down a 'varmint' of a Comanche, burn up his wigwam and its inmates and carry off his mules. He is only a Mexican — a Comanche. But they will not molest the American trader."[21] This observation carried with it no specific suggestion that that prejudicial view was shared by anyone other than the riffraff of the frontier, but perhaps the implication was there of something more widespread.

Certainly the general atmosphere along the western border with regard to Mexico had been adversely affected by the chilling accounts of mistreatment suffered by imprisoned members of the Texan Santa Fe Expedition. Then in May of 1843, while stories of the Chávez case filled the news, word was received on the frontier of the execution of seventeen Texan prisoners of the so-called Mier Expedition, by order of Mexican President Santa Anna. The *New Orleans Bee*, using printer's ink fortified with acid, denounced the act as, perhaps, "the most inhuman piece of butchery that has been perpetrated by a government professing to be civilized within the present century."[22] Such rhetoric, calculated to inflame passions, no doubt had a strong impact upon the thinking of Americans in the West.

The Chávez case also invited invidious comparisons between the United States and Mexico, with regard to notions of justice and the functioning of their respective judicial systems. A case in point involved the murder of an American trader, Andrew Daley, in New Mexico during the winter of 1838. Gregg relates that "The assassins were arrested, when they confessed their guilt; but, in a short time, they were permitted to run at large, in violation of every principle of justice and humanity."[23] As a result, he says, merchants in Santa Fe lodged a protest with Governor Armijo, who at first threatened the petitioners for their temerity, but then, having second thoughts, placed the murderers in nominal imprisonment for a year or two. U.S. Consul Alvarez, in fact, notified Washington at the end of 1842 that the killers of Daley "had been set at liberty by the authorities of Santa Fe, without any trial or punishment whatever."[24] All that, intoned Gregg, "contrasts very strikingly with the manner our courts of justice have since dealt with those who killed Chávez."[25]

The fact was that the prevailing sentiment in Missouri largely reflected that expressed by Audubon — the McDaniel gang should be punished to the full extent of the law for its crime, Texas commissions and Chávez's Mexican nationality notwithstanding. Conviction seemed certain for not only were there confessions, but the Chávez servants had been found wandering on the plains and brought into the settlements to stand witness. After remaining in Independence a short time, they were sent on to St. Louis.

The next legal action in the case, so far as is known, occurred in early July. Judge Catron, traveling on circuit, arrived back in St. Louis to find that defendant John McCormick, one of those with the Prefontaine party, had made application to bail. He decided that as the crime of robbery and murder was punishable with death upon conviction, no application to bail any of the parties would be received by him. Observed the press: "The judge, by this, appears to make no distinction, and will without doubt arraign them all for murder."[26]

That did not happen, however. By the time a special session of the Circuit Court had been convened by Judge Robert W. Wells in Jefferson City the following September, a division was made between those who had remained with McDaniel and participated in the slaying, and those who had decamped with Dr. Prefontaine prior to the act. The latter group was indicted for larceny only. But the grand jury found indictments against the entire company for illegally organizing a military expedition on American soil. Interesting to note, Clay County Clerk Abraham Shaffer was also indicted under a charge of "misprision of felony," meaning that while not an accessory, he had failed in his official duty to notify of a felony.[27]

The indictments were filed on 16 September 1843. On the 25th of the same month the court handed down a startling ruling with regard to Chávez's servants. "On account of the inability of [José] Dolores Perea, Juan J. Bayegos, José J. Bayegos, Juan García to give security in recognizance for their attendance as witnesses on behalf of the United States gainst John McDaniel, David McDaniel, Joseph Brown and Thomas Towson (Indicted for murder) at the next term of the Circuit Court of the United States for the District of Missouri, to be held at the city of St. Louis in and for said district on the first Monday of April next — it is ordered by the court that Dolores Perea, Juan J. Bayegos, José J. Ballegos, Juan García be committed to prison [in the original the words *in the custody of* have been scratched out and replaced by *to prison*] by the Marshall of the district for safe keeping."[28]

Although by this the wretched survivors of the tragic episode were ordered imprisoned for six months to insure their presence at the coming trial, records reveal that compensation was provided them with payment of $362.75 each for 229 days attendance on court and five cents per mile for their return travel to Santa Fe.[29] Gregg mentions "five Mexicans who were with Chávez" having been rescued from the plains, and newspaper accounts also speak of five.[30] Thus, by the court order citing only four, one remains unnamed and unaccounted for.

In the wake of the indictments, Dr. Prefontaine and his associates, Nathaniel Morton, John McCormack, William F. Harris, and Samuel O. Berry, were speedily brought to trial in Jefferson City on the charge of larceny. The jury returned a verdict of guilty in the doctor's case,

TO THE PUBLIC.

The many incorrect versions which have been circulated concerning what occurred at my office on the 26th ult., render it necessary that I should give an explanation of my course to the public. In doing so, however, it is not my intention to notice in detail all the various and contradictory stories afloat, but to confine myself to such as to the candid and just may appear important, and it is to the candid and just only that I shall undertake to offer any appeal.

It is known that on the t day John McDaniel made his appearance in Liberty, and in less than an hour afterwards was seized by some citizens of Jackson upon a charge of murder. A short time after he was released, but, having attempted to escape, was pursued, re-taken, and delivered to the custody of his pursuers from the other side of the river. It is also known that a large amount of gold and silver bullion and gold dust was found in the clerk's office.

In reference to the finding of the money, I have this to say. McDaniel, Judge Thompson and myself were in the office, when the citizens from Jackson approached the door to which McDaniel had just advanced, and seized him. The Judge and myself immediately left the office, and as soon as McDaniel was disarmed, and those who had him in custody had got out, I locked the door. About an hour afterwards I was sent for while at Mr. Tillery's office. When I arrived at the corner of my office, I was addressed by Mr. S. B. Green, whose tone and manner did not please me, and from whose language I inferred that he meant to charge me with being connected with McDaniel. So strongly was I impressed with this idea, that I at once replied in substance, as well as I now recollect, as follows—"I do not wish to hear such imputations, & if your object is, as it seems, to make testimony against me, you shall not enter my office except with legal authority." I then walked a few steps from the door, when Dr. Moss as well as Mr. Green having assured me that nothing of the kind was intended, I then remarked that I would not open the door to the crowd, but that any two or three gentlemen might go in, and suggested Dr. Moss and Judge Thompson, who, in conjunction with Dr. Wood and the sheriff, Mr. Baxter, made the examination. What transpired during that examination I am willing that those gentlemen should state, and the conclusions which they came to I am not disposed to shrink from. My hesitation for a few moments in giving those gentlemen the key of the wardrobe where McDaniel had deposited his effects, the character of which I knew not, for I had not thought of examining them, will be censured by my friends, and readily seized hold of by my enemies for the purpose of doing me serious injury. This, I admit, was imprudent on my part and an error of judgment; I am nevertheless unconscious that any moral guilt attaches to me in the affair, and however my motives may be misconstrued, I have the satisfaction to be able to say with truth, that my own conscience does not reproach me; nor am I without a firm reliance on the impartial good sense of a reflecting community whose favor I have long enjoyed, and in whose opinion it has been my pride to have stood heretofore with a reputation, so far as I know, without a blemish.

Another circumstance to which, I have understood, a false coloring has been given, is my having, after the search had terminated, instituted an examination in the wardrobe and found an amount of gold bullion and gold dust, which, it is said, I did not deliver until the next morning, as if those who are disposed to calumniate me, imagined there was some heinous offence in such delay. The fact is simply, that I deemed it due to myself, and to the cause of justice, to examine the wardrobe myself more carefully, upon doing which I found the gold, much the larger por-

tion of McDaniel's booty, and on the same evening placed it in the custody of Mr. Samuel Tillery.

It has been intimated to me, also, that I am censured for allowing McDaniel to come to my office at all on his return. To those who remember the position he occupied in society here before and up to the very moment of his departure, being generally received and treated with respect and courtesy, and that others of our citizens whose respectability can not be questioned met him quite as cordially as I did, this will appear indeed a very frivolous and pitiable objection. It will appear still more so, when it is recollected that I, in common, I believe, with the rest of the community, had ample reason to think and did think, from flying rumors and the plausible story told by Berry (who returned some three or four days before McDaniel,) that the expedition had not reached its destination, and turned out to be a complete failure. I am fully persuaded that to impartial men many reasons will readily occur why I should not have expelled a young man from my office with whom I had been acquainted for many years, before I knew that he had committed any offence against the laws of the country.

But I have to meet a still graver charge, which I fear has been the chief source of the denunciation which has visited me, and arises from a loan of about fifty dollars which it is said I made to McDaniel before he left here. From this circumstance, I am informed, it is contended that I was to share in the profits of his rash and criminal act, and that his object in returning direct to this town was to make the division with me. The absurdity of basing such a superstructure on so slight a foundation must at the first glance strike every mind endued with common sense, particularly when it is known to a number of respectable citizens in town that McDaniel's name was entered on the steamboat register for St. Louis, that he did not intend to stop at Liberty, and only did so because he ascertained as the boat passed Ducker's landing, that he would be intercepted at the lower landing. I will state what I know, and all I know about McDaniel's expedition. I had always understood that his object was to go to the northwestern limits of Texas, where he expected to join Col. Warfield, and in conjunction with him retaliate on Mexican citizens the outrages which the latter have so often perpetrated upon Texians. He always disavowed to me, and I presume to every other citizen, the intention of committing any act of hostility against Mexicans or any other persons within the territory of the U. States, nor did I ever suppose he would be guilty of an act of this description. In the expedition itself, whatever may have been its object, I had no interest, and expected nothing from it. The advance of 50 dollars which I made to him on the eve of his starting, was made with the view of inducing him to secure to me about one hundred and fifty dollars which I had advanced to him long before, all which with the fifty dollars last advanced he did secure, as far as the nature of the case would admit of, by a power of attorney to receive the same from the trustee under the will made by William McDaniel in favor of John McDaniel. It would be a very erroneous supposition, and one unjust to me, that I expected him to pay what he owed me out of the proceeds either of his Lilliputian warfare upon Mexico, or any other source, except from that before mentioned. So far from having such an expectation, I never entertained any idea that he would return to this country.

It may be that I have not noticed all the charges and perversions to which this unfortunate transaction has given birth. I have aimed to meet all that have come to my ear that may weigh against me with any who have been my friends heretofore, and whom it would be ungrateful and unnatural not to wish to retain. In conclusion I will repeat, that I rely on the consciousness I have that in this affair I have violated no moral duty, and confidently appeal to the justice of the people of Clay county.

Abraham Shaffer.

Liberty, May 1, 1843.

Clay County Clerk Abraham Shaffer's broadside defending his actions in the McDaniel case. (Missouri Historical Society, St. Louis) but recommended mercy. As a result, he was fined one thousand dollars and given a year in prison. In the other four cases, the jury failed to agree, so Judge Wells ordered the defendants to appear for new trials in April. As John McDaniel and the others accused of murder were then unprepared for their defense, he also set their trial dates for April, in St. Louis.[31]

There exists a curious footnote to the later career of Dr. Prefontaine who was the most substantial of those entangled in the crime. It comes from a Captain James Hobbs whose autobiography, first published in 1873, relates a long series of adventures in the West. At first glance, Hobbs's account appears more imaginative than real, yet at least some of it is based on solid fact. Inasmuch as his narrative supplies historical details available nowhere else, it is worth the effort to try and segregate out what is true. That is especially the case with what he has to say about Dr. Prefontaine.

According to Captain Hobbs, he was hunting along the Pawnee Fork in central Kansas in the spring of 1843 with a party out of Bent's Fort. Unexpectedly, soldiers from Fort Leavenworth appeared with word of the recent murder of Chávez. They were pursuing the culprits, accompanied by one of the servants who had escaped to the fort and alerted the authorities. When the commander learned that Hobbs and his men knew the country, they were enlisted to join in the quest for the murderers.

"After four day's search, aided by the teamster [read, servant], we met this band of robbers, who little dreamed of an attack by government troops. They attempted to escape, but I shot Prefonton's (sic) horse from under him, and a soldier shot one of the band named Asbury, when the party surrendered. . . . Dr. Prefonton escaped the gallows by turning state's evidence, and was sent to the penitentiary, from which after serving two years, he was pardoned."[32]

As already noted, Josiah Gregg, usually regarded as a reliable source, presents a very different version of the capture of Prefontaine, claiming that it was effected by Nicholas Gentry heading a ten-man posse. Gregg refers to Daniel Yoacham as accompanying the doctor back toward Council Grove to recover the buried loot and makes no mention of anyone named Asbury.[33] One other independent document, however, does include the name Asbury, so in fact Captain Hobbs may have been correct about his presence.[34] But whether the captain actually shot Prefontaine's horse from under him, or for that matter was even personally involved in the capture, as he claims, remains a matter for speculation.

The important point here is that Hobbs, by whatever manner, does seem to have come face to face with the doctor in 1843. That is confirmed by the fact that many years later he recognized him upon a chance meeting in the lobby of the El Dorado Hotel in San Francisco. As the captain soon learned, Prefontaine was residing in that city and editing a paper, mainly devoted to scandal.

"When he [Prefontaine] saw me standing conversing with a party of gentlemen, he eyed me for some time; and when a favorable opportunity presented, inquired if we had not met somewhere before. I asked him if he remembered how I shot his horse on the plains after the murder of Charvis and party; which caused him to turn deathly pale, and he begged me not to expose him. He said he was now leading an honest life and was managing the publication of a paper. I told him to have no fears of my exposing him, so long as he behaved himself; but should he pursue the opposite course, he might expect me to reveal his former character. I often met him afterwards in San Francisco, but he never was easy in my presence. He died in Oakland few years ago, leaving a family; and I am not aware that anyone in those parts ever found out his true character or connection with the aforesaid murder."[35]

The trials of the remaining nine defendants began at St. Louis on 1 April 1844, with Judges Wells and Catron jointly presiding. During the weeks that followed, the cases of the four men charged only with larceny were disposed of with considerable dispatch. Harris and McCormick plead guilty and, upon recommendation of the United States attorney, William M. McPherson, who noted that they were poor, were fined ten dollars and sentenced to nine months' imprisonment. Morton, convicted on the sixteenth, received the same penalty. Charges against Berry were dropped for turning state's evidence, and he was released on 18 May.[36]

These mild sentences can perhaps be explained by the action of Attorney McPherson who had decided to concentrate his attention upon a zealous prosecution of the five men charged with the killing. Their trials, as the *St. Louis Democrat* reported, "produced great excitement."[37] And it is clear that it was the wish of the general populace and the intention of the court to make an example of them.

In the course of the proceedings, a number of Americans involved in the Santa Fe trade were called as witnesses, among them John C. Mc-Coy and Nicholas Gentry.[38] Also receiving subpoenas were Samuel C. Owens and Robert Aull, both prominent merchants of Independence. Owens, in addition, was the clerk of the Jackson County Court. They had taken charge of the Chávez plunder upon arrest of the gang. With opening of the trials they were ordered to St. Louis, and in the words of the subpoenas, "there to bring into said court the following articles, to wit, one large piece of silver bullion weighing about sixty-nine pounds [This had been taken from John McDaniel upon his arrest in Liberty.], one leather purse of gold dust weighing four pounds and some ounces, a quantity of old silver, one piece of gold bullion weighing about one pound and a half, and one medal, the property of the late Antonio José Chávez to be used in evidence."[39]

Some of the most valuable testimony was that provided by the Chávez servants. Since none were conversant in English, the court engaged in interpreter. He was Rice Patterson who had made eight trips over the Santa Fe Trail beginning in 1826 and had enjoyed a three-year residence in New Mexico. As a result of his experience, he was both fluent and literate in Spanish.[40]

The translated statement of José Dolores Perea was virtually the same as that of the other three servants. He testified that on the fatal morning they were eating breakfast when John McDaniel and four of his men escorted Chávez from camp. Upon hearing a gunshot, Perea recalled, "we raised up . . . & saw the deceased running & the others in pursuit. . . ." The guards commanded the servants to sit down, so that they did not actually see the slaying. But shortly the accused men returned to camp with some of Don Antonio's personal valuables.[41]

The direction taken by the defense attorney, Edward Bates, was that, first, the attack upon Chávez was mitigated by John McDaniel's Texas commission. But Judge Wells disposed of that argument since no such commission had been produced, and even if it had, he made clear, the document could not have excused homicide. So a second line, one that attempted to discredit the chief witnesses for the prosecution, was pressed with full vigor by Bates. Chiefly, he directed his attack at William Mason, the man abandoned by the McDaniels on the steamer *Weston* and the one who was first to confess the crime. The McDaniels and Brown denounced him as "a perjured villain" and "a vile miscreant who unscrupulously fabricated the basest falsehoods to secure his own safety at the expense of the lives of his associates."[42] And, indeed, the defense counsel was able to introduce outside evidence confirming the witness's unreliable character.

However, Mason's description of the shooting of Chávez, which has been presented in an earlier chapter, was substantiated by the testimony of old Thomas Towson. It received further support from the statements of the Mexican servants, which Attorney Bates was unable to discredit. In a desperate bid to exonerate himself, John McDaniel tried to shift the burden of guilt to Mason, and also to Gallatin Searcy, an ardent Texas patriot, who, he claimed, had first suggested killing Chávez. McDaniel's own version of the incident is contained in an interview granted after the trial.

In that he declared: "About an hour after these seven men had been gone [the Prefontaine party], Chavis asked me to walk out with him [apparently to relieve himself]. I complied, and as we started, I told four men to go to work at the packs. Chavis and I walked about 100 yards beyond where the packs laid, when I stopped and Chavis went on some 15 or 20 steps further and he stopped. I turned around to speak to the men at the packs, and while thus engaged giving directions, Brown looking towards me hallowed out, 'Chavis is running.'

"I wheeled about, and as I turned, drew a pistol from my belt and fired towards Chavis and ordered him to stop, and then hallowed to the men to catch him, starting in a run after him myself. As the men came running, they fired their pistols. After running about 100 yards, I caught Chavis, and in catching him we both fell, I falling a step or two ahead. At the very moment that I had arisen got back to the side of Chavis, who had also got upon his feet, Brown and Mason came running up, each with a pistol in his hand presented.

"As Brown, who was 3 or 4 feet ahead of Mason, came in my reach, I struck his pistol down and cried out, 'Don't shoot,' but by the time these words were fairly spoken, Mason's pistol fired, the ball of which hit Chavis in the back part of his head and killed him instantly. I immediately aimed a blow at Mason, which he dodged, almost entirely escaping its intended effect. At this instant, my brother and G. Searcy came up and took hold of me and requested me not to strike Mason anymore. With this request, I complied, but in language abused Mason severely, until he asked my pardon and declared, that when he shot he scarcely knew what he was doing.

"To satisfy Mason that he alone had killed or wounded Chavis, we examined the body carefully and there was no other wound on it than the one made by Mason. It was in the course of this examination that we found a belt containing thirty-nine doubloons. Having nothing with which to dig a grave, we put the body in the creek."[43]

By this remarkably contrived tale did John McDaniel not only endeavor to excuse his actions and point the finger of culpability elsewhere — principally to Mason — but he went so far as to try and make himself the hero of the piece. His words were carefully gauged for maximum effect upon listeners, for example, his reference to having "put" the body of Chávez in the creek. Every other account declares that the body was callously "thrown" into the creek, that being a much stronger verb than "put." In any event, the juries bought none of it, and all four men — the McDaniels, Brown, and Towson — were found guilty, and the first three were condemned to the gallows. Judgment on Towson was suspended, as he was considered mentally defective. Mason would have probably received the death sentence had he not turned state's evidence. As it was, the United States attorney declined to prosecute him.

The last verdict, the one against Joseph Brown, was returned on 27 April. The composure he had maintained throughout his trial gave way and a journalist among the spectators described him as "very much affected." Anticipating the verdict, he read a prepared statement to the jury, asking its members to intercede in his behalf with the president. The McDaniel brothers also made a similar request, at the same time protesting their innocence.[44] The court set the following 14 June as the date of execution.

The harsh sentences were greeted with warm approval across the state of Missouri. When word of the crime had first been learned, the frontier press was loud in its warnings that if the government failed to take energetic measures to bring the outlaw gang to account, then the lucrative Santa Fe trade might be utterly destroyed.[45] That fear, coupled with a commendable devotion to the securing of justice, had animated the posses in a diligent pursuit of the offenders. After the trials, the *St. Louis Democrat*, calling the Chávez killing "as base and dastardly murder as was ever perpetrated," reminded readers that parties to the important Santa Fe traffic had a right to the protection of our laws, adding that "a powerful, solemn admonition is required; something that shall be *effectual* to prevent the recurrence of such crimes."[46] The admonition it favored was the carrying out of the death sentences. Therefore, the paper urged rejection of pleas for pardon or commutation, an act that would represent, in its opinion, "mistaken mercy, in no way subservient to the true ends of justice."[47]

No sooner had the verdicts been handed down than the defense lawyer filed for a new trial on the grounds that the U.S. Circuit Court lacked jurisdiction in murder cases arising in the Indian country. He concluded that this represented "the first time that criminal jurisdiction has been assumed by a federal court without an express statutory grant."[48] The matter was given some review by Judges Wells and Catron. Years later John C. McCoy, Westport's founder and stellar citizen, would claim that he was one of those called to St. Louis "as a witness to prove jurisdiction of the court."[49] Presumably, his part merely required testimony establishing that the crime had indeed taken place beyond Missouri's western boundary. In the end, the two judges denied the challenge by the defense and reaffirmed jurisdiction of the Circuit Court.

Quickly, the condemned men, their families and friends sent the first of a series of messengers to Washington to lay appeals for clemency before President John Tyler. While awaiting the answer, Joseph Brown from his cell undertook to write a sketch of his life. About that, one editor commented: "From the intelligence he displayed during his trial, we are led to judge that it will be a weak written document; but the conclusion is a sorry story for a man to close his biography with."[50]

During this same period, a young man studying for the ministry visited the prisoners. He asked John McDaniel if he did not "acknowledge the justice of the sentence and was prepared to submit to the stern dictates of the law?" The reply he received cut short his visit, for McDaniel flew into a rage and only the strength of the iron door prevented him from committing another murder. The press suggested that "such unthinking and imprudent students should be prevented from making visits."[51]

President Tyler granted a stay of execution for John McDaniel and Joseph Brown until 12 July and a longer one, until 27 June 1845, for the younger McDaniel and Thomas Towson, the latter also having been assigned the death penalty.[52] Regarding David McDaniel and Towson, the first reports mistakenly claimed that they had been pardoned. Incensed over the apparent presidential show of mercy, *Niles National Register*, sometimes characterized as the *Time* magazine of its day, declared: "It would really seem as if we are soon to have no longer an inducement to be bothered with the forms of courts and expense of trial. They are certainly useless, if the guilty are so invariably pardoned."[53] Shortly, however, the error was discovered and the paper issued a correction.[54]

After another appeal to the president, the execution date was again delayed, this time to 16 August. Once more an envoy was hurried to Washington while John McDaniel and Brown nervously watched the approach of the dreaded day. Meanwhile, work began on the construction of a gallows at the army arsenal located two miles south of St. Louis near the riverbank.[55] Citizens regularly scanned the newspapers, expecting any day an announcement that a new reprieve, or even a pardon, would be forthcoming from Washington.

The sixteenth arrived, however, without further word from President Tyler, so the fate of McDaniel and Brown was sealed. U.S. Marshal Weston F. Birch had charge of the execution, and at two o'clock in the afternoon he removed them from their cells. Escorted by a detachment of German dragoons, the condemned men were conducted to the arsenal. The party was accompanied by several thousand spectators on foot and horseback and consisting of men, women and children. The throng would have been larger, but many St. Louis residents stayed home believing that a reprieve would arrive at the last minute and the hanging would be called off.[56]

The scaffold had been built several hundred yards west of the arsenal. Marshal Birch led McDaniel and Brown up the steps and then read their death sentences in front of the assembled multitude. As was the custom of the time, each man delivered a brief, final speech, incidentally, still protesting their innocence. Then the trap was sprung and they paid for the murder of Antonio José Chávez with their lives.[57]

The reprieve granted to David McDaniel and Thomas Towson proved their salvation, for afterward on 22 October pardons for both were received from President Tyler. By then the executions had cooled popular passions and the rhetoric in the press, so that sentiment now favored leniency for the remaining two men. Owing to the youth of David McDaniel and the age and mental condition of Towson, the pair were conceded to have been the misguided pawns of gang leader John McDaniel. The charity also was extended to those who had been convicted of larceny, for they received presidential pardons at the same time.[58] Although the sorrowful incident was closed, it was not soon forgotten by any of those associated with the Santa Fe trade.

said David C. McDaniel, until the
twenty-first day of June 1845.

In testimony whereof, I have
hereunto subscribed
my name and caused
the seal of the United
States to be affixed.
Done at the City of
Washington, this 21st.
day of June, A.D.,
1844; and of the In-
dependence of the United
States of America the
Sixty eighth.

John Tyler

By the President:
J. C. Calhoun
Secretary of State.

Last page of the presidential reprieve for David McDaniel. (Missouri Historical Society, St. Louis)

AFTERMATH

THE SPILLING of Antonio José Chávez's blood in April of 1843 was just the first in a long train of violent incidents that marred life on the trail for the remainder of that year. Some of what happened was a direct consequence of his case, while other events, originating quite independently, afterward became intertwined in the myriad of threads representing spinoffs from the murder. In the larger view, the troubles of '43 were all closely tied to stresses in the Santa Fe trade imposed by the conflict between Texas and Mexico, with the United States caught in the unenviable middle.

During the months the McDaniel gang was awaiting trial, Colonel Charles Warfield had been manfully striving to carry out his visionary plans. Upon leaving Independence the previous October, he had traveled up the Arkansas River to the southern Rockies where he spent the winter recruiting men for his proposed campaign against New Mexico. The few trappers he managed to enlist were told to meet at the mouth of the Purgatory near Bent's Fort early the next March. At the appointed time, a scant twenty-four volunteers, bearded and ill-clothed, put in an appearance. Dismayed by the poor showing, Warfield, nevertheless, appointed officers and organized his spindly ranks. Then, after sending ten of the men scouting toward the New Mexican settlements, he led the remainder down the Arkansas River to his rendezvous at Point of Rocks where he expected to meet the forces coming from Missouri and Texas.

It was reports of these activities reaching New Mexico that had aroused the fears of government officials and traders and had prompted Antonio José Chávez, when he left for Missouri, to take the more southerly Cimarron Cutoff. Governor Armijo heard of Warfield from the alcalde of Taos, who got the news by way of men drifting down from the mountains.[1] As a result of the threat, the annual east-bound caravan which departed on 1 April also chose to follow the Cimarron route.

Colonel Warfield, arriving at the Point of Rocks several weeks after Chávez had passed went into camp to await the arrival of his "main army." He had no way of knowing that the Missouri contingent, even smaller in numbers than his own, was already under arrest on a charge of murder. And the force from Texas, which he was counting on to form the main muscle, was nowhere in evidence. After a decent lapse of days convinced him that he was alone in the venture, he turned west again, guiding his followers to a reunion with the scouting party at the Rabbit Ears, a major Santa Fe Trail landmark in northeastern New Mexico.

From there, the Warfield party rode on toward the New Mexican settlements, although it was now obvious to all that the colonel's vaunted plan to conquer the province had dissolved. Still, he was determined to strike some blow, ineffectual though it must be. Approaching the town of Mora, on a branch of the trail, a Mexican troop was attacked and scattered leaving five dead on the field. Following this utterly pointless affray, Warfield ordered a withdrawal eastward. But soon after, while he was camped near the Wagon Mound, Mexican cavalry in pursuit managed to run off all the horses. Left afoot, the dejected freebooters were obliged to walk two hundred miles north to Bent's Fort on the Arkansas. Once arrived, the colonel disbanded his men and made preparations to leave for Texas. All of his exertions had produced nothing but a fiasco.[2]

The conclusion of this episode, however, saw the gate open upon another. The chief player in the next chapter was Colonel Jacob Snively who in February had received a commission from Texas, much like that granted to Warfield the year before, to intercept Mexican caravans on the Santa Fe Trail. Gathering 190 men in a unit grandly named the "Battalion of Invincibles," Snively crossed the Red River on

25 April and by late May he was bivouacked at a major caravan crossing on the Arkansas, not far from Warfield's rendezvous at Point of Rocks. Was Snively's battalion the force Warfield had been expecting from Texas? There is nothing in the available record to suggest that the two men had any prior contact with one another, or that Snively when he rode north was looking for Warfield, but such may have been the case. Arguing against it is the fact that Colonel Warfield, returning down the Arkansas following the disbanding of his own unit, fell in with the Invincibles and at once placed himself under the command of Snively. He would hardly have taken that step had this been the army he was anticipating.

For the next several weeks, the Texans waited impatiently on the river. Rumor had led them to believe that the spring caravan from Missouri was composed mainly of Mexicans who had wintered in the states, and they meant to seize and plunder it. They may have also gotten wind that much of the freight was consigned to that arch foe of Texas, Governor Manuel Armijo. From a supply train owned by the American proprietors of Bent's Fort, which rumbled by and was accorded safe passage, two pieces of information were acquired. One was the story of the Chávez murder and the apprehension of the parties responsible — so at last Colonel Warfield learned the outcome of his alliance with John McDaniel. The other news, more critical to the business at hand, was that Governor Armijo in his concern over the safety of the incoming caravan was marching out from Santa Fe with six hundred soldiers to meet it at the international boundary, the Arkansas.[3]

To forestall Armijo's interference with his attack on the approaching Mexican merchants, Colonel Snively dispatched Warfield with some of the Invincibles to try and delay the Governor's progress. Taking the Cimarron Cutoff south of the river, Warfield had moved across the open plain only about fifteen miles when he encountered an advance party of one hundred militiamen under Captain Ventura Lovato. A pitched battle followed resulting in the capture or killing of all but two men who fled back to Armijo. When the governor learned of the defeat he immediately retreated to Santa Fe.[4]

For another week Snively continued to cool his heels on the Arkansas. When at the end of that time his scouts returned from a downriver look and reported no trace of a caravan, a portion of his restless men decided they had seen enough. On the following day some seventy-odd members of the command took their leave and started back to Texas.

That left Snively with a force of only 107, but still adequate, he concluded, to handily capture any size wagon train that might yet show up. The one thing he had not counted on was companies of U.S. dragoons escorting the caravan.

It will be recalled that earlier the concern over the first tidings of the Warfield and McDaniel missions had moved Colonel Kearny to order out troops from Forts Leavenworth and Scott to protect the spring train to Santa Fe. It was after that that the commotion over the Chávez murder broke, and when shortly it was learned that a Colonel Snively from Texas was moving north to pose a new menace to the trail, the escort duty assigned the dragoons assumed added significance. Indeed, some writers have declared that the stern action United States soldiers later took against Snively's Invincibles was a direct response to the slaying of Chávez.[5]

Command of the escort was given to Captain Philip St. George Cooke. On 27 May he rode out of Fort Leavenworth and took to the Santa Fe Trail ahead of the caravan. With him were three companies of dragoons, 160 strong.[6]

On 13 June Cooke reached the vicinity of the Great Bend of the Arkansas where his path chanced to cross that of a separate patrol from Fort Gibson (in present eastern Oklahoma). It was under the charge of Captain Nathan Boone, youngest son of Daniel Boone. The previous day, Boone relates in his official journal, he and his men had come upon "the Santa Fe trace at a place which I call'd Mulberry grove, and in this grove, I found the encampment of the party which rob'd and murdered C. Garvis [Chávez], the Spaniard. . . . I searched for the remains of C. Garvis & also sent out two detachments in search of those who had lately been there, but could find neither."[7] After remaining with Cooke several days, Boone turned southwest toward the Canadian River.

On the last day of the month, Captain Cooke with his formidable ranks surprised the Texans in their camp situated seven or eight miles west of the one hundredth meridian and thus inside U.S. territory. The captain remarks in his own journal that he had met Snively before, back in 1836 at Nacogdoches, Texas, where he (Snively) "was a shopkeeper's clerk, and quite insignificant in appearance and demeanor."[8] This second encounter in no way improved Cooke's opinion of the man. Following a stiff argument over whether the camp was on American soil or on land claimed by Texas, Captain Cooke settled the matter by disarming the Invincibles and announcing that their foray was over. Afterward he allowed them to march back to Texas.[9]

The disturbances on the Santa Fe Trail in the spring and summer of 1843, beginning with the death of Chávez and continuing through the collapse of the Snively Expedition, affrighted officials in Mexico City. Initially, they had only the sketchiest details of the circumstances, but what was known persuaded them that Texas was moving toward a full-scale invasion of New Mexico, with encouragement if not direct aid from the United States.[10] It was that apprehension in part that brought President Santa Anna to issue a drastic decree on 7 August. Thereby, the customs houses in New Mexico, including the one at El Paso, were ordered closed to Americans and the overland commerce with the United States by way of the Santa Fe Trail was suspended. Another motive that prompted this act was the president's anger over corruption among New Mexican customs officials who routinely connived with American merchants to smuggle in contraband goods.[11]

The shock this prohibition produced on the Missouri frontier can scarcely be overestimated. The state's economy had become so firmly bound to the trade with Santa Fe that its termination seemed to guarantee financial ruin for a large segment of the mercantile class. Nor was the dismay any less in New Mexico and Chihuahua where local fortunes were dependent upon business with the United States. Influential native merchants at Santa Fe threatened to take the side of Texas unless the 7 August decree was repealed, and American observers acquainted with the situation there predicted a revolution if the customs houses remained closed.[12]

While much of this could be dismissed as hollow bluster, there is no question that the president's punitive act stirred up a storm. Not only that, it came at a time when people in Santa Fe were suddenly warmer toward Americans. Their attitude had been decidedly hostile earlier in the year after news filtered in from the trail of the loss of Antonio José Chávez. But then it softened when notice of the arrest of the killers was received. However, the greatest elation was displayed upon the news of Cooke's triumph over the Invincibles. That stunning announcement, quoting an eastern paper, "is reported to have had a powerful influence over the Mexicans when it reached Santa Fe, which they exhibited by treating the Americans with much hospitality and kindness, instead of the ill-will which had previously marked their intercourse."[13]

Ultimately, the same news also produced a favorable reaction in

President Santa Anna. He had been slow to receive accurate intelligence of the state of affairs along his northern frontier, but as the picture began to be clarified, matters did not appear so grim. He may have heard of the arrest of the McDaniel gang, and that would have had a positive effect. But the turning back of Snively's Texans on the Arkansas made the strongest impression. He is reputed to have declared that "it was the first time the United States had shown a friendly spirit toward Mexico."[14]

Whether because of that, or owing to the clamor and protests coming from his subjects in New Mexico, Santa Anna on 31 March 1844 abolished his earlier decree and reopened the ports of entry in the north to foreign trade. Official notification of that step was promptly sent to the State Department in Washington.[15] At once Missouri merchants rushed to purchase goods and outfit their wagons for a season on the trail they had thought would not come. With the resumption of overland commerce and the execution of John McDaniel and Joseph Brown that same summer, the curtain can be considered to have closed upon the historical drama begun when Don Antonio José Chávez bid his last farewell to New Mexico and pointed his mule teams eastward toward Missouri.

Several footnotes remain to be added to the story. In the years after 1843, Owl Creek took the name of the man who had died there. But that name, so unfamiliar to frontier folk knowing no Spanish, became hopelessly mangled — Chavis, Chauvey, Charvis, Garvis, Jarvis, and so forth. But at last Jarvis was settled upon and by that name is the creek shown on all maps today.

Sometime after the murder, relatives or friends of the victim coming from New Mexico paused long enough to erect a marker in his memory at the approximate site of the tragedy. This could have been Don Antonio's brother José who is known to have made almost yearly crossings to Independence and Westport during the latter 1840s and early 1850s. Or the marker could have been installed afterward by nephews who inherited the family freighting business. Whoever assumed the task would have had to expend more than casual effort. A pioneer homesteader in remembering it, described the marker as a shaft of solid rock some seven or eight feet tall by two feet wide. Carved upon its face was the single word "Chávez." The nearest stone suitable for quarrying such a piece lay ten miles to the east on bluffs overlooking the Little Arkansas.[16]

Doubtless, nothing more than a commemorative monument was intended, but many passersby thought it a grave and so identified it in their trail diaries or journals. By the end of the century, the marker had vanished, probably carried off by some farmer to use as a fence corner, foundation stone, or doorstep. With it went the last physical trace recalling how Jarvis Creek got its name.

Even before the monument was erected, travelers to and from Santa Fe would halt at the site and reflect upon the tragedy. Captain St. George Cooke, escorting a second caravan in September of 1843, came to the place on a phantasmal evening and painted the scene in gloomy terms. "The cold north wind, laden with ceaseless rain, moans dismally through the dank cottonwoods; dark, deep beneath, through its slimy banks creeps the sullen stream. . . . 'Twas *here* that a cry to God, wrested by human fiends from a brother man, fell unanswered, — echoless on the desert air. . . . Here, without a tear, a word, a look of human sympathy, was poor Charvis deliberately murdered."[17] Others, while less effusive in recording the experience, were nonetheless moved by recollection of this fragment of history. Before long, however, the chronicle of Chávez and his lamentable end became much garbled and a body of folklore grew around it. Prominent in that vein was a tale that the outlaw gang had buried and never recovered a portion of Don Antonio's gold and silver. To this day the lost treasure yarn occasionally surfaces and, we can presume, leads to furtive digging in the wheat fields now along Jarvis Creek.[18]

Of the relatives of Chávez, who may have contributed to the monumenting of his memory, a final few words can be said. It is recorded that Mariano Chávez, filled with resentment, blamed all foreigners — presumably Americans — for the deed that claimed his brother's life.[19] Frank S. Edwards, a volunteer in the army that conquered New Mexico in 1846, wrote at an overnight camp on Jarvis Creek: "The place we are now is the same where the trader Chavis was so brutally murdered in 1843, by a party of land pirates. His grave lies just outside the belt of timber which skirts the stream. [So the marker seems to have been placed by that date.] I, afterwards, while in New Mexico, met with a young son of Chavis', about eleven years old, who had come to our camp to get medical advice for an uncle. In the course of conversation we asked him, knowing that he had been educated at St. Louis, how he liked Americans? His little eyes glittered, as he exclaimed, 'When I am a man, I shall be a soldier; and then I'll kill every American I can. They murdered my father, and I'll pay them for it!'"[20] A nice story, but it

José Francisco Chávez, nephew of Antonio José Chávez. As a boy he accompanied the spring caravan, 1843, to Missouri. (Museum of New Mexico Neg. No. 27132)

cannot be accurate. Don Antonio's only son, José Feliciano, was five years old in 1846, not eleven, so it is unlikely that he delivered such a speech and impossible that he had been to St. Louis to school. If it actually occurred, the speaker must have been one of the nephews, perhaps José Francisco.

Another soldier at this time, Private John T. Hughes, suggests a different attitude for the Chávezes. Marching with his company down the Rio Grande from Albuquerque, he passed Peralta, close to the hacienda of Los Padillas. "This town," he says, "is the place of residence of the Chávez family, the brothers and relations of the Chávez who was murdered by Capt. McDaniel's band of marauders. . . . They are wealthy, and have chiefly educated their sons in the United States. They are friends to the Americans."[21] By now, Mariano was dead, and it may well be, as Hughes indicates, other family members had gotten over the bitterness caused by the loss of Don Antonio. Or if not, they were keeping quiet about it, with an American army occupying their country.

The uncle referred to above, in need of medical advice from the passing U.S. Army, was José Chávez, then the last survivor of the three original Chávez brothers. In fact, his need for the services of a physician was urgent. As another soldier informs us: "The old gentleman . . . brother of the one killed near the frontier of Missouri some years ago . . . had both his arms broken by a fall from a mule."[22] The limbs must have mended satisfactorily for José was soon back in the Santa Fe trade, making his annual visits to Missouri. But, not surprisingly, he seems to have been stalked by a fear of highway robbers.

His anxiety was particularly acute in 1849 when he set out with a reputed one hundred thousand dollars in Mexican silver sewn up in large rawhide pouches. En route he had the good fortune to fall in with well-known freighter Francois X. Aubry who was traveling in the same direction. Aubry, by agreeing to provide protection on the trail, persuaded Chávez to change his destination from Independence, where the New Mexicans were accustomed to do business, to the village of Westport, the residence of some of Aubry's friends in the outfitting trade. One of those friends, William R. Bernard, would affirm years later that the subsequent "transaction with Chávez, more than any other, brought the Mexican trade to Westport and Kansas City," especially when it became known "that they could meet all the requirements here."[23]

The wagon jockey box that carried Don Antonio's treasure. Now in a private collection, Albuquerque. (Author's photo)

And a final note: Following the murder trials, the money and personal possessions that had belonged to Don Antonio were again placed in the hands of Jackson County clerk and Santa Fe trader Samuel Owen for return to the Chávez family, with whom he was well acquainted. He entrusted the actual task to his good friend Dr. Henry Connelly of Liberty, Missouri, then a resident of New Mexico who was preparing to depart for Santa Fe. Connelly carried out the charge as requested and in the process became taken with the charms of Dolores Perea de Chávez. In 1849, four years after the death of her husband, Mariano, they were married. He afterward made a name for himself as the Civil War governor of New Mexico and died in 1866.[24]

Under circumstances not clear, Don Antonio's wagon looted on Owl Creek was recovered and also returned to the Chávezes in New Mexico. It stayed in the family until recent years when it was sold to a collector. The best preserved part of the vehicle was the wagon jockey box that had carried the principal part of the treasure. That box, in its way, remains as the most haunting momento of an evil day long ago on the Santa Fe Trail.

NOTES

INTRODUCTION

1. Maurice Garland Fulton, ed., *Diary & Letters of Josiah Gregg*, 2 vols. (Norman: University of Oklahoma Press, 1941-1944), 1:124.

2. Lyn McDaniel, ed., *Bicentennial Boonslick History* (Boonville, Mo.: Boonslick Historical Society, 1976), 66-67. *Niles National Register*, 17 June 1843, suggested, "If the year 1843 escapes the prediction of father Miller, and is not rendered memorable as 'the year of the great comet,' . . . it will at least be remembered as 'the year of the locusts.'" A brief summary of Millerism is available in J. C. Furnas, *The Americans, A Social History* (New York: G. P. Putnam's Sons, 1969), 502.

3. *Missouri Intelligencer*, 14 April and 19 June 1826.

4. See, for example, Josiah Gregg, *Commerce of the Prairies*, ed. Max L. Moorhead (Norman: University of Oklahoma Press, 1954), 332n. On the same matter Dragoon Captain Philip St. George Cooke wrote, also in 1843, "The trade is falling into the hands of the Mexicans: of about 200 wagon loads which I have escorted this year, I do not believe *ten* have belonged to Americans who were resident citizens." William E. Connelley, ed., "A Journal of the Santa Fe Trail," *Mississippi Valley Historical Review* 12 (June 1925): 254.

5. Max L. Moorhead, *New Mexico's Royal Road* (Norman: University of Oklahoma Press, 1958), 188-89.

I. THE VICTIM

1. Fray Angelico Chávez, *Origins of New Mexico Families* (Santa Fe: Historical Society of New Mexico, 1954), 323. Gregg, *Commerce of the Prairies*, 341. In a personal conversation with the author, in 1980, genealogist Fray Angelico Chávez described the church archives for the towns south of Albuquerque as containing serious gaps for the early nineteenth century, particularly in the record of births and marriages.

2. For background on Chávez family history in New Mexico, see Chávez, *Origins of New Mexico Families*, 18-23, 160-64, 321-26; Marc Simmons, *The Little Lion of the Southwest* (Chicago: Swallow Press, 1973), 11-22.

3. Ralph Emerson Twitchell, *The Leading Facts of New Mexican History*, 2 vols. (Albuquerque: Horn and Wallace, 1963), 2:25-26.

4. Donald Dreesen, "Genealogical Notebooks," unpaginated manuscript, Special Collections, Coronado Room, University of New Mexico Library, Albuquerque. See entry for Mariano José Chávez y Castillo.

5. Ibid.; Ward Alan Minge, "Frontier Problems in New Mexico Preceding the Mexican War, 1840-1846" (Ph.D. diss., University of New Mexico, 1965), 157.

6. Ibid, 159, 167; Lawrence R. Murphy, "The Beaubien and Miranda Land Grant, 1841-1846," *New Mexico Historical Review*, 42 (January 1967): 33.

7. Dreesen, "Genealogical Notebooks." See entry for José Antonio Chávez y Castillo. Also, Chávez, *Origins of New Mexico Families*, 323-24.

8. Susan Shelby Magoffin, *Down the Santa Fe Trail and Into Mexico*, ed. Stella M. Drumm (New Haven: Yale University Press, 1926), 154.

9. Gregg, *Commerce of the Prairies*, 134. John O. Baxter, "Las Carneradas: New Mexico's Sheep Trade to Chihuahua and Durango Before 1846" (M.S. thesis, University of New Mexico, 1982), 99.

10. Minge, "Frontier Problems," 172; Bills of Indictment in the Chávez case, Special Session of the U.S. Circuit Court, District of Missouri, 16 September 1843, Federal Archives and Research Center, Kansas City, Mo. [FARC].

11. Moorhead, *New Mexico's Royal Road*, 195; W. H. H. Allison, "Colonel Francisco Perea," *Old Santa Fe*, 1 (October 1913): 213; David Alex Sandoval, "Trade and the Manito Society in New Mexico, 1821-1848" (Ph.D. diss., University of Utah, 1978), 197. The eastern firms often honored drafts between traders and performed other "banking" services for their convenience. See, for example: Peter Harmony, New York, receipt for Manuel Alvarez, payment to Antonio José Chávez of $377.50, 9 [May?] 1842. Alvarez Papers, Folder no. 13, New Mexico State Records Center and Archives, Santa Fe [NMSRCA].

12. John E. Sunder, ed., *Matt Field on the Santa Fe Trail* (Norman: University of Oklahoma Press, 1960), 51, 291.

13. *Niles National Register*, 30 November 1839.

14. *New Orleans Daily Picayune*, 12 June 1840.

15. Acting U.S. Consul Manuel Alvarez to Secretary of State Daniel Webster, Washington, 2 February 1842, Despatches from U.S Consuls in Santa Fe, 1830-1846, Record Group 59, microcopy no. 199, roll 1, National Archives, Washington, D.C. (hereafter cited as Despatches from U.S. Consuls). Also, Louise Barry, *The Beginning of the West* (Topeka: Kansas State Historical Society, 1972), 383, 410.

16. *New Orleans Daily Picayune*, 25 May 1840. Also, Guías and Tornaguías, 1840, Mexican Archives of New Mexico, NMSRCA.

17. Ibid. For detailed explanation of the nature of the *guías*, see Moorhead, *New Mexico's Royal Road*, 139. Minge, "Frontier Problems," 113.

18. For example of items numbered among the *efectos del país*, see Hacienda Records, Libro de Guías, Santa Fe, 1844, Mexican Archives of New Mexico, NMSRCA.

19. Gilberto Expinosa and Tibo J. Chávez, *El Rio Abajo* (Pampa, Texas: Pampa Print Shop, 1973), 157.

20. The expedition was represented by Texans as a peaceful trading party and by Mexico as a hostile invasion. Its story is related in all general histories of the region. A thorough-going study is provided by Noel M. Loomis, *The Texas-Santa Fé Pioneers* (Norman: University of Oklahoma Press, 1958).

21. Barry, *The Beginning of the West*, 449.

22. Alvarez to the Secretary of State, Independence, 1 July 1843, Despatches from U.S. Consuls.

23. Ibid.

24. *Commerce of the Prairies*, 337.

25. Ibid., 341.

26. Ibid.

27. Claims Against Mexico, Claim no. 66 of Manuel Alvarez, et al., 1842, Santa Fe, Records of the Department of State, National Archives.

28. *New Orleans Weekly Picayune*, 22 May 1843.

29. *Commerce of the Prairies*, 337.

30. *St. Louis New Era*, 29 April 1843.

31. Howard Louis Conrad, *"Uncle Dick" Wootton* (Chicago: W. E. Dibble & Company, 1890), 22.

32. *The Old Santa Fe Trail* (Topeka: Crane & Company, 1899), 97.

33. Alvarez to the Secretary of State, Washington, 2 February 1842, Despatches from U.S. Consuls.

II. THE PLOT

1. Quoted in Henry P. Walker, "A Texas Gamble, The Snively Expedition of 1843," *The Smoke Signal* [Tucson Corral of the Westerners], no. 42 (Fall 1981), 20.

2. *New Orleans Weekly Picayune*, 1 May 1843.

3. John Francis McDermott, ed., *Travels in Search of the Elephant: The Wanderings of Alfred S. Waugh* (St. Louis: Missouri Historical Society, 1951), 4-5. For biographical sketches of Warfield, see Janet Lecompte, *Pueblo, Hardscrabble, Greenhorn* (Norman: University of Oklahoma Press, 1978), 98-99; H. Bailey Carroll, "Charles A. Warfield," in Walter Prescott Webb, ed., *Handbook of Texas*, 2 vols (Austin: Texas State Historical Association, 1952), 2: 862-63; Nicholas P. Hardeman, "Charles A. Warfield," in LeRoy R. Hafen, ed., *The Mountain Men and the Fur Trade of the Far West*, 10 vols. (Glendale: The Arthur H. Clark Company, 1965-1972), 7: 353-69.

4. Seymour V. Connor, *Adventure in Glory, The Saga of Texas, 1836-1849* (Austin: Steck-Vaughn Company, 1965), 201-3.

5. Ibid., 202.

6. Hockley to Warfield, 16 August 1842, Senate Exec. Docs., 32d Cong., 2d sess. (Serial 660), no. 14, 117-18.

7. W. Eugene Hollon and Ruth L. Butler, eds., *William Bollaert's Texas* (Norman: University of Oklahoma Press, 1956), 143.

8. William Campbell Binkley, *The Expansionist Movement in Texas, 1836-1850* (Berkeley: University of California Press, 1925), 108.

9. *St. Louis New Era*, 21 April 1843.

10. Lecompte, *Pueblo, Hardscrabble, Greenhorn*, 99.

11. *New Orleans Weekly Picayune*, 1 May 1843. The paper reported that according to rumor General Hugh McLeod, former commander of the Texan Santa Fe Expedition would be leading the wing from Texas, composed of 150 men, to meet Warfield in the

spring. It discounted the rumor, however, because McLeod was then visiting in Georgia, not recruiting troops in the Republic.

12. Names of participants in the gang, with variations in spelling and form, can be found in: Account of Josiah Gregg published in the 27 May 1843 issue of the [Van Buren] *Arkansas Intelligencer*, and reprinted in Maurice Garland Fulton and Paul Horgan, eds., *New Mexico's Own Chronicle* (Dallas: Banks Upshaw Company, 1937), 132; also, Bills of Indictment in the Chávez case, Special Session of the U.S. Circuit Court, District of Missouri, 16 September 1843, FARC; and, *Niles National Register*, 10 June 1843; and, *Missouri Republican* [St. Louis], 2 May 1843. The Harris brothers may have been among the several sons of Ruben Harris, an early pioneer of Independence who owned a horse-mill. See Anonymous, *The History of Jackson County, Missouri* (Kansas City: Union Historical Company, 1881), 297, 368.

13. William G. B. Carson, ed., "The Diary of Mat Field," *Bulletin, Missouri Historical Society*, 5 (April 1949): 167n.

14. Zealia B. Bishop, "The Earliest Fur Traders and Merchants," *Westport Historical Quarterly*, 2 (August 1966): 6; William A. Goff, *Old Westport* (Kansas City: privately printed, 1977), 61.

15. The Chávez Gold, unsigned manuscript in Snyder Papers, no. 3524, f153, Western Historical Manuscript Collection, State Historical Society of Missouri, University of Missouri, Columbia.

16. Barry, *The Beginning of the West*, 380, 412-13.

17. Conrad, *"Uncle Dick" Wootton*, 23.

18. Quoted in *Niles National Register*, 10 June 1843.

19. Goff, *Old Westport*, 61-62.

20. The Chávez Gold, 1.

21. Early Westport merchant William R. Bernard in his recollections identifies "the Yocum tavern" as McDaniel's rendezvous. "Westport and the Santa Fe Trade," *Transactions, Kansas State Historical Society*, 9 (Topeka, 1906): 553.

22. The best source on Yoacham and his tavern is Adrienne Christopher, "Daniel Yoacham, Pioneer Innkeeper of Westport," *Westport Historical Quarterly*, 1 (November 1965): 3-8. The author, a direct descendant of Daniel, states therein (p. 7), "It was at the Yoacham Tavern that the robbers met, unknown to Yoacham." See also, "Recollections of Susannah Yoacham Dillion," Ibid., 9-12, wherein Daniel's daughter informs us that he was known as "honest squire Yoacham" (p. 10). Other references to John McDaniel's presence at the tavern can be found in Goff, *Old Westport*, 60-61; Bishop, "The Earliest Fur Traders and Merchants," 8.

23. Inman, *The Old Santa Fe Trail*, 98.

24. Conrad, *"Uncle Dick" Wootton*, 23.

25. A somewhat different version of the departure is given by pioneer John C. McCoy who said that the company was "gotten up and fitted out very secretly at Liberty. . . . They crossed the river at the ferry at Kansas City, remained one day near Westport and left." *Kansas City Journal*, 23 January 1879. His statement does not preclude McDaniel's being in Westport and at Yoacham's Tavern off and on during the previous months.

III. THE CRIME

1. Barry, *The Beginning of the West*, 468.

2. Mitchell to Porter, St. Louis, 21 April 1843, Senate Exec. Docs., 32d Cong., 2d sess. (Serial 660), no. 14, 112-13.

3. Fayette Copeland, *Kendall of the Picayune* (Norman: University of Oklahoma Press, 1943), 96n.

4. Alvarez to the Secretary of State, Independence, 1 July 1843, Despatches from U.S. Consuls. See also, Barry, *The Beginning of the West*, 455.

5. *New Orleans Weekly Picayune*, 24 April 1843.

6. *St. Louis New Era*, 21 April 1843.

7. *New Orleans Weekly Picayune*, 24 April 1843.

8. *Niles National Register*, 10 June 1843.

9. *Kansas City Journal*, 23 January 1879. In this issue John Calvin McCoy, founder of Westport, refers in his recollections to the Chávez killing as having occurred on Owl Creek. Afterward that stream was known as Chávez (Jarvis) Creek, as will be explained below. Randolph B. Marcy in his *The Prairie Traveler* (New York: Harper & Brothers, 1859), 261 and 298, locates Owl (or Charez [sic]) Creek just over ten miles west of the Little Arkansas Crossing. Those accounts that place the murder on Little Cow Creek or on Cow Creek, the next two crossings on the trail, are clearly in error.

10. Barry, *The Beginning of the West*, 469.

11. *Arkansas Intelligencer*, 27 May 1843.

12. From the *St. Louis New Era*, quoted in *Niles National Register*, 10 June 1843. According to writer Larry D. Ball, John McDaniel originally assured his subordinates he would turn Chávez over to Texan officials. Later, at his trial McDaniel claimed, among a welter of conflicting statements, that the shooting that followed had been accidental. See, Ball, "Federal Justice on the Santa Fe Trail: The Murder of Antonio José Chávez," *Missouri Historical Review* 81 (October 1986): 3.

13. *Arkansas Intelligencer*, 27 May 1843.

14. Ibid.; *St. Louis Democrat*, 30 April 1844.

15. From the *St. Louis Republican*, quoted in *New Orleans Weekly Picayune*, 6 May 1844.

16. Ibid.

17. *Niles National Register*, 10 June 1843.

18. W.L. Webb, *The Centennial History of Independence, Missouri* (Independence: privately printed, 1927), 229.

19. *Boonville* [Missouri] *Observer*, 8 May 1844.

20. *Arkansas Intelligencer*, 27 May 1843.

21. *Commerce of the Prairies*, 138.

22. *Arkansas Intelligencer*, 27 May 1843.

23. Conrad, "Uncle Dick" Wootton, 23.

IV. THE CHASE

1. Richard Gentry, *The Gentry Family in America* (New York: Grafton Press, 1909), 76-77, 156. Reference courtesy of Pauline Fowler.

2. David J. Weber, ed. and trans., *The Extranjeros, Selected Documents From the Mexican Side of the Santa Fe Trail, 1825-1844* (Santa Fe: Stagecoach Press, 1967), 17.

3. James Josiah Webb, *Adventures in the Santa Fe Trade, 1844-1847* (Glendale: The Arthur H. Clark Company, 1931), 81.

4. *Kansas City Journal*, 23 January 1879.

5. Gentry, *The Gentry Family in America*, 156. A lengthy biographical sketch of Reuben Gentry appeared under the title, "An Old Timer," in the *Santa Fe New Mexican Review*, 27 September 1883, on the occasion of his return visit to Santa Fe late in life. The

Petition to Daniel Webster, Santa Fe, 16 September 1841, is preserved in the Read Collection, no. 9A NMSRCA.

6. *Santa Fe New Mexican Review*, 27 September 1883.

7. *Arkansas Intelligencer*, 27 May 1843.

8. Barry, *The Beginning of the West*, 468.

9. *Commerce of the Prairies*, 338; and, Barry, *The Beginning of the West*, 468.

10. Quoted in the *New Orleans Weekly Picayune*, 15 May 1843.

11. Order printed in ibid., 24 April 1843.

12. Quoted in *Niles National Register*, 13 May 1843.

13. Ibid.

14. Hardeman, "Charles A. Warfield," 357.

15. Henry Pickering Walker, *The Wagonmasters* (Norman: University of Oklahoma Press, 1966), 144.

16. *Niles National Register*, 20 May 1843; and, *New Orleans Weekly Picayune*, 29 May 1843.

17. Report from its correspondent in Independence, dated 20 April, appearing in *Missouri Republican*, 28 April 1843.

18. Goff, *Old Westport*, 60; and, Christopher, "Daniel Yoacham," 7.

19. Anonymous, *The History of Jackson County, Missouri*, 643; and, Bernard, "Westport and the Santa Fe Trade," 553.

20. A useful biographical sketch of Gilpin appears in William Elsey Connelley, *Doniphan's Expedition* (Topeka: privately printed, 1907), 552-65. A standard biography is Thomas L. Karnes, *William Gilpin, Western Nationalist* (Austin: University of Texas Press, 1970).

21. *Arkansas Intelligencer*, 27 May 1843.

22. Karnes, *William Gilpin*, 81n.

23. *Missouri Republican*, 29 April 1843.

24. Events associated with the voyage of the *Weston* from Fort Leavenworth to Owens Landing, as related in the preceding paragraphs, are drawn mainly from Gregg's account in the *Arkansas Intelligencer*, 27 May 1843; some details come from the *Missouri Republican*, 29 April 1843 and from the privately printed broadside by Abraham Shaffer, issued at Liberty, Missouri, 1 May 1843, a copy of which is in the Santa Fe Trail file, Missouri Historical Society, St. Louis.

25. *Missouri Republican*, 29 April 1843; and, *St. Louis New Era*, 29 April 1843.

26. "Missouri River Steamboats," *Transactions, Kansas State Historical Society*, 9 (1906): 312.

27. Shaffer, "To the Public" [privately printed broadside cited in note 24 above].

28. *Missouri Republican*, 3 May 1843.

29. Shaffer, "To the Public." There is a discrepancy in the dates here that cannot be easily resolved. Mason, according to press reports, was taken at Owens Landing on 24 April and the posse seems to have crossed the river and entered Liberty on the same day. Earlier that morning the McDaniels had jumped the *Weston* and by all accounts suffered arrest soon afterward. Yet, Shaffer, an eye-witness to events, states that the confrontation at his office between the posse and John McDaniel transpired on 26 April, providing an unexplained gap of two days.

30. 3 May 1843.

31. The seven preceding paragraphs are based on Shaffer's broadside, "To the Public."

32. Bills of Indictment in the Chávez case, Special Session of the U.S. Circuit Court, District of Missouri, 16 September 1843, FARC.

33. *Arkansas Intelligencer*, 27 May 1843. Other accounts place the figure as high as five thousand dollars. See, for example, *Niles National Register*, 13 May 1843.

34. *Missouri Republican*, 27 April 1843.

35. Ibid., 3 May 1843.

36. *St. Louis Reporter*, 1 May 1843.

37. Pearl G. Wilcox, *Jackson County Pioneers* (Independence, Mo.: privately printed, 1975), 214.

38. *Arkansas Intelligencer*, 27 May 1843; and, *St. Louis Gazette*, 10 May 1843.

39. *Arkansas Intelligencer*, 27 May 1843. Peyton and an unnamed brother were suspected of being parties to the Chávez robbery, but they were never tried. One of them soon after went to California and returned to Missouri wealthy. This, according to a letter, S. B. Harvey to S. J. Spear, Emporia, Kansas, 10 February 1903, copy in possession of the Kansas State Historical Society, Topeka.

40. *Arkansas Intelligencer*, 27 May 1843.

41. Ibid. The court later placed a value of $13,620 upon Chávez's property. Ball, "Federal Justice on the Santa Fe Trail," 11.

42. 3 May 1843.

V. THE TRIAL

1. Fulton, *Diary & Letters of Josiah Gregg*, 1:17.

2. Ibid., 1:125n.

3. For reference to this issue of the *Arkansas Intelligencer* and to the reprint of Gregg's article taken from it, see Chapter II, note 12, above. References to the murder in *Commerce of the Prairies* can be found scattered through pp. 337-44.

4. *Missouri Republican*, 3 May 1843.

5. Webb, *The Centennial History of Independence*, 229.

6. John Francis McDermott, ed., *Audubon in the West* (Norman: University of Oklahoma Press, 1965), 80.

7. Bernard, "Westport and the Santa Fe Trade," 553.

8. Ball, "Federal Justice on the Santa Fe Trail," 10.

9. *St. Louis New Era*, 3 May 1843.

10. *New Orleans Weekly Picayune*, 22 May 1843.

11. Christopher, "Daniel Yoacham," 7.

12. Bernard, "Westport and the Santa Fe Trade," 558.

13. *Niles National Register*, 3 June 1843.

14. *St. Louis New Era*, 3 May 1843.

15. Ibid., 1 May 1843, quoted in *New Orleans Weekly Picayune*, 15 May 1843.

16. *New Orleans Weekly Picayune*, 15 May 1843.

17. Quoted in *Niles National Register*, 3 June 1843.

18. Leroy R. Hafen and Ann W. Hafen, eds., *Rufus B. Sage, His Letters and Papers, 1836-1847*, 2 vols. (Glendale: The Arthur H. Clark Company, 1956), 2:281.

19. *St. Louis New Era*, 29 April 1843.

20. Van Zandt to Upshur, 4 August 1843, Senate Exec. Docs., 32d Cong., 2d sess. (Serial 660), no. 14, 117.

21. *New York Common Advocate*, quoted in *Niles National Register*, 10 June 1843.

22. *New Orleans Bee*, 4 May 1843.

23. *Commerce of the Prairies*, 262-63.

24. Alvarez to the Secretary of State, 1 July 1843, Despatches from U.S. Consuls, in which reference is made to Alvarez's note to the secretary of 18 December 1842. Preliminary judicial proceedings against the Daley murderers, Salbador Barela and Diego Martín, 1 March-31 August 1838, are contained in the Mexican Archives of New Mexico, microfilm roll 25, frames 72-214, NMSRCA.

25. *Commerce of the Prairies*, 263. Gregg reiterated the point later in his book, 344, wherein he declares, "But witness the active exertions on the border to bring these depredators [the McDaniel gang] to justice — and then let the contrast be noted betwixt this affair and the impunity with which robberies are everyday committed throughout Mexico. . . ." His statement was a rebuttal to an official protest lodged by the Mexican Minister of Foreign Affairs, José María de Bocanegra, against American outlaws. The minister's letter was published in *Niles National Register*, 16 September 1843.

26. Ibid., 8 July 1843.

27. Bills of Indictment in the Chávez case, Special Session of the U.S. Circuit Court, District of Missouri, 16 September 1843, FARC. All fifteen gang members were named in the indictments, although, as observed, five had successfully evaded capture.

28. Ruling on the Chávez servants, 25 September 1843, in Ibid. The name "Bayegos" must have been improperly rendered by the court. The original could have been "Gallegos," a common surname in New Mexico. Or, more likely, it was "Ballejos," a family name linked by marriage to the Chávezes south of Albuquerque.

29. Ball, "Federal Justice on the Santa Fe Trail," 7.

30. *Arkansas Intelligencer*, 27 May 1843.

31. *Niles National Register*, 7 October 1843; and Ball, "Federal Justice on the Santa Fe Trail," 4.

32. James Hobbs, *Wild Life in the Far West* (Hartford: Wiley, Waterman & Eaton, 1873), 465-66.

33. *Arkansas Intelligencer*, 27 May 1843.

34. Undated note regarding the men involved in the Chávez murder, Snyder Papers, no. 3524, f153, Western Historical Manuscript Collection, State Historical Society of Missouri, University of Missouri, Columbia. William Gilpin in several instances provides corroboration for Hobbs' story. For example, he too says that Chávez's servant(s) brought in word of the killing and claims to have gone in pursuit as far as present-day Dodge City, that is, beyond the Pawnee Fork. Gilpin is thought to have headed a twenty-man posse, but there is some suggestion that his enterprise was associated with dragoons which, if so, fits in with the Hobbs account. However, Gilpin makes no mention of Hobbs or capture of the Prefontaine party, so after all it is difficult to give the captain's recital much credit, at least as far as his own role was concerned. See, Karnes, *William Gilpin*, 81.

35. Hobbs, *Wild Life in the Far West*, 466-67.

36. *New Orleans Weekly Picayune*, 29 April 1844; and, Ball, "Federal Justice on the Santa Fe Trail," 11.

37. 23 April 1844.

38. *Kansas City Journal*, 23 January 1879.

39. Record of Owens and Aull subpoenas, St. Louis, 25 September 1843, FARC. See also, Goff, *Old Westport*, 61.

40. The reference to Patterson and his identity as the court interpreter was provided by his great-grandson in a personal letter to the author, Thad Patterson to Marc Simmons,

Seagraves, Texas, 1 December 1984. The *St. Louis Democrat*, in its edition of 23 April 1844, reported that "The Spaniards gave their testimony yesterday."

41. Ball, "Federal Justice on the Santa Fe Trail," 6-7.

42. *St. Louis Democrat*, 30 April 1844; and, *New Orleans Weekly Picayune*, 6 May 1844. For other accusations against Mason, see, Ball, "Federal Justice on the Santa Fe Trail," 7.

43. *Boonville* [Missouri] *Observer*, 8 May 1844.

44. *New Orleans Weekly Picayune*, 6 May 1844.

45. *Missouri Republican*, 29 April 1844.

46. *St. Louis Democrat*, 30 April 1844.

47. Ibid.

48. Ball, "Federal Justice on the Santa Fe Trail," 11.

49. *Kansas City Journal*, 23 January 1879.

50. *St. Louis Republican*, 28 May 1844, as quoted in the *Missouri Register* [Boonville], 4 June 1844.

51. Ibid.

52. See, President's respite of John McDaniel and Joseph Brown, until Friday, 12 July 1844; Death warrants for Joseph Brown and David McDaniel, August 1844; all on file in FARC. A duplicate copy of the respite for David McDaniel, signed by the president, 21 June 1844, is in the collections of the Missouri Historical Society, St. Louis.

53. 29 June 1844.

54. *Niles National Register*, 13 July 1844.

55. On the arsenal, see, Alphonso Wetmore, *Gazetteer of the State of Missouri* (St. Louis: C. Keemle, 1837), 213.

56. *St. Louis Democrat*, 17 August 1844.

57. *Missouri Register*, 27 August 1844; Certificate of Execution, by U.S. Marshal Weston F. Birch, 16 August 1844, attached to Death Warrant of Joseph Brown, in FARC. Several details of the execution are contained in Thomas James, *Three Years Among the Indians and Mexicans* (reprint ed.; Chicago: Rio Grande Press, 1962), 157n.

58. *St. Louis Democrat*, 30 April 1844; and, Ball, "Federal Justice on the Santa Fe Trail," 14.

VI. AFTERMATH

1. Three letters from the alcalde of Taos, describing Warfield's activities, are included in Armijo to the Minister of War and Navy, 22 March-4 April 1843, Mexican Archives of New Mexico, NMSRCA.

2. For an account of the Warfield Expedition by one of the participants, see, Hafen and Hafen, *Rufus B. Sage*, 2: 207-52. A good recent summary is provided by Hardeman, "Charles A. Warfield," 357-64.

3. Ibid., 365-66.

4. The incident is described in Barry, *The Beginning of the West*, 479; Twitchell, *The Leading Facts of New Mexican History*, 2: 85. See also, *Niles National Register*, 26 August 1843. The site of the action became known to Santa Fe Trail travelers as "The Battleground."

5. See, for example, H. Bailey Carroll, "Warfield Expedition," in Webb, *Handbook of Texas*, 2: 863.

6. *Niles National Register*, 1 July 1843. About two weeks before Cooke's departure, the eastbound caravan from Santa Fe that had started 1 April and included Antonio José

Chávez's brother and nephew reached the Missouri frontier, having slipped past before Snively came upon the Santa Fe Trail. It was said to comprise 42 wagons and 180 men and to carry upward of $250,000 in bullion, a rich prize had it fallen into the hands of the Texans. Barry, *The Beginning of the West*, 475-76.

7. Louis Pelzer, *Marches of the Dragoons in the Mississippi Valley* (Iowa City: State Historical Society of Iowa, 1977), 185.

8. Connelley, "A Journal of the Santa Fe Trail," 92.

9. For a contemporary account of the confrontation, see, *St. Louis Republican*, 21 July 1843. Official papers related to the Snively Expedition are contained in George P. Garrison, ed., *Diplomatic Correspondence of the Republic of Texas*, 2 vols. (Washington: Government Printing Office, 1911), 2: 212-21.

10. *El Diario del Gobierno* [Mexico], 19 July 1843.

11. Daniel Tyler, "Gringo Views of Governor Manuel Armijo," *New Mexico Historical Review*, 45 (January 1970): 36. A copy of the decree was printed in *Niles National Register*, 11 November 1843.

12. Ralph P. Bieber, "The Papers of James J. Webb, Santa Fe Merchant, 1844-1861," *Washington University Studies*, 11 (April 1924): 258.

13. *Niles National Register*, 21 October 1843.

14. Cited in Anonymous, "A Privateer of the Western Plains," *Frontier Times*, 12 (October 1934): 40.

15. *Niles National Register*, 29 June 1844.

16. "Jarvis Creek Misnamed," in a scrapbook of undated clippings titled "Rice County Clippings, 1876-1955," vol. 1-2, p. 101, Kansas State Historical Society, Topeka; Horace Jones, *Up From the Sod* (Lyons, Kan.: Rice County Historical Society, 1968), 169-70.

17. Philip St. George Cooke, *Scenes and Adventures in the Army* (Philadelphia: Lindsay & Blakiston, 1857), 249-50.

18. See, for example, the following story which introduces the fanciful twist that Don Antonio himself managed to hide his treasure before capture: "Chávez Buried His Bullion?" in *Hutchinson News Herald*, 28 May 1950.

19. Murphy, "The Beaubien and Miranda Land Grant," 32.

20. Frank S. Edwards, *A Campaign in New Mexico* (Philadelphia: Carey and Hart, 1847), 27.

21. John T. Hughes, *Doniphan's Expedition* (Cincinnati: U. P. James, 1847), 233.

22. "Journal of Marcellus Ball Edwards," in Ralph P. Bieber, ed., *Marching With the Army of the West* (Glendale: The Arthur H. Clark Company, 1936), 211.

23. Bernard, "Westport and the Santa Fe Trade," 557.

24. For a somewhat mangled version of Owen's and Connelly's role in the return of Don Antonio's treasure, see Hobbs, *Wild Life in the Far West*, 466. Also, consult Dreesen, "Genealogical Notebooks," entry for Henry Connelly.

BIBLIOGRAPHY

ARCHIVAL MATERIALS

Kansas State Historical Society, Topeka.
  Rice County Clippings, 1876-1955.
  Santa Fe Trail file.
Missouri Historical Society, St. Louis.
  Santa Fe Trail file.
New Mexico State Records Center and Archive, Santa Fe [NMSRCA].
  Alvarez Papers.
  Mexican Archives of New Mexico.
  Read Collection.
National Archives, Washington, D.C.
  Despatches from U.S. Consuls, Record Group 59.
  Records of the Department of State, 1843-1844.
State Historical Society of Missouri, University of Missouri, Columbia,
  Western Historical Manuscript Collection.
  Snyder Papers.
Federal Archives and Research Center, Kansas City [FARC].
  U.S. Circuit Court Records, District of Missouri, 1843-1844.

NEWSPAPERS

Boonville Observer
El Diario del Gobierno [Mexico City]
Hutchinson News Herald
Kansas City Journal
Missouri Intelligencer
Missouri Register
Missouri Republican
New Orleans Bee
New Orleans Daily Picayune, later the
  New Orleans Weekly Picayune
Niles National Register
Santa Fe New Mexican Review
St. Louis Democrat
St. Louis Gazette
St. Louis New Era
St. Louis Republican

85

UNPUBLISHED STUDIES

Baxter, John O. "Las Carneradas: New Mexico's Sheep Trade to Chihuahua and Durango Before 1846." Master's thesis, University of New Mexico, 1982.

Dreesen, Donald. "Genealogical Notebooks." Special Collections, Coronado Room, University of New Mexico Library, Albuquerque.

Minge, Ward Alan. "Frontier Problems in New Mexico Preceding the Mexican War, 1840-1846." Ph.D. diss., University of New Mexico, 1965.

Sandoval, David Alex. "Trade and the Manito Society in New Mexico, 1821-1848." Ph.D. diss., University of Utah, 1978.

PRINTED SOURCES

Allison, W.H. "Colonel Francisco Perea." *Old Santa Fe* 1 (October 1913): 210-22.

Anonymous. *The History of Jackson County, Missouri.* Kansas City: Union Historical Company, 1881.

————. "A Privateer of the Western Plains." *Frontier Times* 12 (October 1934): 37-40.

Ball, Larry D. "Federal Justice on the Santa Fe Trail; The Murder of Antonio José Chávez." *Missouri Historical Review* 81 (October 1986): 1-17.

Barry, Louise. *The Beginning of the West.* Topeka: Kansas State Historical Society, 1972.

Bernard, William R. "Westport and the Santa Fe Trade." *Transactions, Kansas State Historical Society* 9 (Topeka, 1906): 252-65.

Bieber, Ralph P. "The Papers of James J. Webb, Santa Fe Merchant, 1844-1861." *Washington University Studies* 11 (April 1924): 255-305.

Binkley, William Campbell. *The Expansionist Movement in Texas, 1836-1850.* Berkeley: University of California Press, 1925.

Bishop, Zealia B. "The Earliest Fur Traders." *Westport Historical Quarterly* 2 (August 1966): 3-11.

Carroll, H. Bailey. "Charles A. Warfield." In *Handbook of Texas,* edited by Walter Prescott Webb, 862-63. 2 vols. Austin: Texas State Historical Association, 1952.

Carson, William G. B., ed. "The Diary of Mat Field." *Bulletin, Missouri Historical Society* 5 (April 1949): 157-84.

Chávez, Fray Angelico. *Origins of New Mexico Families.* Santa Fe: Historical Society of New Mexico, 1954.

Christopher, Adrienne. "Daniel Yoacham, Pioneer Innkeeper of Westport." *Westport Historical Quarterly* 1 (November 1965): 3-8.

Connelley, William Elsey. *Doniphan's Expedition.* Topeka: privately printed, 1907.

————, ed. "A Journal of the Santa Fe Trail." *Mississippi Valley Historical Review* 12 (June 1925): 72-98.

Connor, Seymour V. *Adventure in Glory, The Saga of Texas, 1836-1849.* Austin: Steck-Vaughn, 1965.

Conrad, Howard Louis. *"Uncle Dick" Wootton.* Chicago: W. E. Dibble & Company, 1890.

Cooke, Philip St. George. *Scenes and Adventures in the Army.* Philadelphia: Lindsay & Blakiston, 1857.

Copeland, Fayette. *Kendall of the Picayune.* Norman: University of Oklahoma Press, 1943.

Edwards, Frank S. *A Campaign in New Mexico.* Philadelphia: Carey and Hart, 1847.

Edwards, Marcellus Ball. "Journal of . . ." In *Marching With the Army of the West*, edited by Ralph P. Bieber, 107-208. Glendale:The Arthur H. Clark Company, Glendale: 1936.

Espinosa, Gilberto, and Tibo J. Chávez. *El Rio Abajo*. Pampa, Texas: Pampa Print Shop, 1973.

Fulton, Maurice Garland, ed. *Diary & Letters of Josiah Gregg*. 2 vols. Norman: University of Oklahoma Press, 1944.

————— and Paul Horgan, eds. *New Mexico's Own Chronicle*. Dallas: Banks Upshaw Company, 1937.

Furnas, J. C. *The Americans, A Social History of the United States*. New York: G. P. Putnam's Sons, 1969.

Garrison, George P. *Diplomatic Correspondence of the Republic of Texas*. 2 vols. Washington, D.C.: Government Printing Office, 1911.

Gentry, Richard. *The Gentry Family in America*. New York: Grafton Press, 1909.

Goff, William A. *Old Westport*. Kansas City: privately printed, 1977.

Gregg, Josiah. *Commerce of the Prairies*. Edited by Max L. Moorhead. Norman: University of Oklahoma Press, 1954.

Hafen, LeRoy R., and Ann W. Hafen, eds. *Rufus B. Sage, His Letters and Papers, 1836-1847*. 2 vols. Glendale: The Arthur H. Clark Company, 1956.

Hardeman, Nicholas P. "Charles A. Warfield." In *The Mountain Men and the Fur Trade of the Far West*, edited by LeRoy R. Hafen, 7:353-69. Glendale: The Arthur H. Clark Company, 1965-1972.

Hobbs, James. *Wild Life in the Far West*. Hartford: Wiley, Waterman & Eaton, 1873.

Hollon, W. Eugene, and Ruth L. Butler, eds. *William Bollaert's Texas*. Norman: University of Oklahoma Press, 1956.

Hughes, John T. *Doniphan's Expedition*. Cincinnati: U. P. Jones, 1847.

Inman, Henry. *The Old Santa Fe Trail*. Topeka: Crane and Company, 1899.

James, Thomas. *Three Years Among the Indians and Mexicans*. Reprint. Chicago: Rio Grande Press, 1962.

Jones, Horace. *Up From the Sod*. Lyons, Kans.: Rice County Historical Society, 1968.

Karnes, Thomas L. *William Gilpin, Western Nationalist*. Austin: University of Texas Press, 1970.

Lecompte, Janet. *Pueblo, Hardscrabble, Greenhorn*. Norman: University of Oklahoma Press, 1978.

Magoffin, Susan Shelby. *Down the Santa Fe Trail and Into Mexico*, edited by Stella M. Drumm. New Haven: Yale University Press, 1926.

Marcy, Randolph B. *The Prairie Traveler*. New York: Harper & Brothers, 1859.

McDaniel, Lyn, ed. *Bicentennial Boonslick History*. Boonville, Mo.: Boonslick Historical Society, 1976.

McDermott, John Francis, ed. *Audubon in the West*. Norman: University of Oklahoma Press, 1965.

—————, ed. *Travels in Search of the Elephant: The Wanderings of Alfred S. Waugh*. St. Louis: Missouri Historical Society, 1951.

"Missouri River Steamboat." *Transactions, Kansas State Historical Society* 9 (Topeka, 1906): 295-316.

Moorhead, Max L. *New Mexico's Royal Road*. Norman: University of Oklahoma Press, 1958.

Murphy, Lawrence B. "The Beaubien and Miranda Land Grant, 1841-1846." *New Mexico Historical Review* 42 (January 1967): 22-47.

Pelzer, Louis. *Marches of the Dragoons in the Mississippi Valley.* Iowa City: Historical Society of Iowa, 1917.

"Recollections of Susannah Yoacham Dillion." *Westport Historical Quarterly* 1 (November 1965): 9-12.

Senate Executive Documents, 32d Congress, 2d Session (Serial 660), no. 14.

Simmons, Marc. *The Little Lion of the Southwest.* Chicago: Swallow Press, 1973.

Sunder, John E., ed. *Matt Field on the Santa Fe Trail.* Norman: University of Oklahoma Press, 1960.

Twitchell, Ralph Emerson. *The Leading Facts of New Mexican History.* Facsimile ed. 2 vols. Albuquerque: Horn and Wallace, 1963.

Tyler, Daniel. "Gringo Views of Manuel Armijo." *New Mexico Historical Review* 45 (January 1970): 23-46.

Walker, Henry P. "A Texas Gamble, The Snively Expedition of 1843." *The Smoke Signal* [Tucson Corral of the Westerners] 42 (Fall 1981): 17-31.

_____. *The Wagonmasters.* Norman: University of Oklahoma Press, 1966.

Webb, James Josiah. *Adventures in the Santa Fe Trade, 1844-1847.* Glendale: The Arthur H. Clark Company, 1931.

Webb, W. L. *The Centennial History of Independence, Missouri.* Independence: privately printed, 1927.

Weber, David J., ed. and trans. *The Extranjeros, Selected Documents From the Mexican Side of the Santa Fe Trail, 1825-1844.* Santa Fe: Stagecoach Press, 1967.

Wetmore, Alphonso, *Gazetteer of the State of Missouri.* St. Louis: C. Keemle, 1837.

Wilcox, Pearl G. *Jackson County Pioneers.* Independence: privately printed, 1975.

INDEX

ABOUT THE AUTHOR

MARC SIMMONS is a professional historian and author of many books about the Southwest, especially the Indian and Hispanic heritages of New Mexico. He is also recognized as an authority on the history of the Santa Fe Trail.

Dr. Simmons received his higher education at the University of Texas at Austin, the University of New Mexico, and Guanajuato University, Mexico. He has taught at New Mexico, St. John's College, and Colorado College.

A member of Western Writers of America, he received the Golden Spur Award from them in 1983 for his history of Albuquerque. He served for ten years on the New Mexico Governor's Cultural Properties Review Committee for historic preservation and also is a member of the Author's Guild.

Among his twenty books and monographs on Southwestern history are *New Mexico, A Bicentennial History; Following the Santa Fe Trail, A Guide*, and *Alongside the Santa Fe Trail: An Excursion into the Past.*